NEW MUSEUMS IN CHINA

NEW MUSEUMS IN CHINA

CLARE JACOBSON

PRINCETON ARCHITECTURAL PRESS
NEW YORK

TO RICHARD

CONTENTS

NORTHEAST AND NORTH

1
2

3

8 7 5 4
   6

10
23   9

24

11 12
    14 13   EAST
    15 16

25
28 27 26
      29
            21

22

NORTHWEST AND SOUTHWEST

31   30

20 17
19 18

SOUTH CENTRAL

From the twenty-fifth-floor window of my home in downtown Shanghai, I watch the construction of the Shanghai Nature Museum. It looks to be shaping up well, its gracefully curved wall now breaking out of the ground. In another time and another place, this museum would be big news. But today in Shanghai, it is just one of many similar stories. As I am sending this manuscript to press, three major museums have just opened in town: the China Art Museum (the largest museum in China, for the moment), the Long Museum (China's largest private art museum), and the Power Station of Art (the first state-owned museum dedicated to contemporary art).[1] If all goes as planned, ten museums—including the Shanghai Textile Museum, the Changfeng Yacht Exhibition Hall, and the Jackie Chan Museum—will be open in 2013 in the former factory buildings along Suzhou Creek.[2]

Move beyond Shanghai, and the numbers are even more staggering. According to the National Bureau of Statistics, the People's Republic of China (PRC) had 2,571 museums at the end of 2011, which is 1,198 more than in 2000.[3] Chen Jianming, a vice-chairman of the Chinese Society of Museums, stated that 395 museums were built in 2011 alone.[4] And the State Administration of Cultural Heritage said in 2012 that the country had 3,400 museums.[5] We could question the accuracy of these numbers. We might also note that institutions such as the Beijing Museum of Tap Water, the Shanghai Museum of Public Security, and the China Paocai [Pickle] Museum in Meishan, Sichuan, pad the count out a bit.[6] Yet the numbers do speak to the importance that China is placing on museum building. These numbers pale in comparison to the estimated 17,500 museums in the United States.[7] But the rate of their construction in the midst of a global recession that has inhibited museum building in other parts of the world is noteworthy.

It is not mere happenstance that so many new museums are being built in China. Jane Perlez writes in the *New York Times*, "The boom in museum construction, which some Chinese art experts liken to the expansion of museums in the United States at the end of the 19th century, has much to do with national pride. It comes with the full support of the national government."[8] In the seven years leading up to the Beijing 2008 Olympic Games, funding for museum work in the capital quadrupled.[9] And from 2008 to 2010 the central government supported museums with RMB 5.2 billion (USD 803.9 million), according to Chinese sources.[10]

While the most-publicized new museums exist in China's main urban centers, museum building is a nationwide phenomenon. Consider the newly opened Russian People Museum in Enhe in the far

north of Inner Mongolia.[11] This small town has little else to offer tourists, save for a couple of souvenir shops and a Russian bakery. But it seems to have decided that a timber-frame museum exhibiting some traditional farming equipment, a few busts of Vladimir Lenin, and a Russian version of an Elton John album would be enough to draw a crowd. Enhe is not the only town to feel this way. One architect working in China said that museums are "the Louis Vuitton bags of architecture. Every city in China wants one now."[12] Attempts to reproduce the "Bilbao effect"—the rejuvenation of a city through museum building, following Frank Gehry's successful 1997 Guggenheim Museum Bilbao—are everywhere in China.[13]

Numbers alone do not speak of the significance of this building boom. New museums in China are not simply anonymous buildings; they are designed to make a statement. A museum might be built to designate the heart of a new town, or it might witness that an industrial center aspires to be a cultural center, or it might suggest that a once-private art collection is ready to open up to a community. Then again, it might be built for a less altruistic purpose, such as establishing a politician's mark on his territory or increasing the value of a neighboring housing complex.[14] While the idea of architecture as icon has long been under question, more often than not new museums in China are designed to be iconic. They make a statement both physically and symbolically. They are China's new face of culture to the world.

There may be questions about how well these many buildings work as museums, but there is little doubt that they work wonderfully as examples of creative and innovative architectural design. The opportunity to work on museum projects has attracted an amazing group of designers from both China and abroad. Eight Pritzker Prize–winning architects have built or are building new museums in China, and the prize's 2012 recipient, Wang Shu, is best known for his museum design.[15] At the same time, many young firms in China are establishing and promoting their practices with museum work.

Museum buildings, devoid of many of the restraints of residential or office buildings, allow for a rich variety of ideas and forms. Some new museums have idealized shapes, as in the work of Zaha Hadid and Studio Pei-Zhu. Others are driven by local context and history, as are those of Jiakun Architects and Atelier FCJZ. Still others are designed as opportunities for structural and material exploration, such as the museums of Sutherland Hussey and Rocco Design. Not every building is a stand-alone icon. In some cases, new museums fit themselves into China's existing building stock. Arata Isozaki built a new museum in a shopping mall in Shanghai, SOM placed one in a skyscraper in Beijing, Rem Koolhaas added one at the top of a residential tower in Guangzhou, and Neri&Hu put one inside a hotel in Xi'an.

Long Museum,
Zhong Song,
Shanghai, 2012

The fifty-one buildings featured in this book represent the breadth and depth of new museums in China. Each tells a unique story of a specific locale and an inspired designer. Together, the museums mark a ten-year period of influential new architecture. Frank Krueger, creative director of the firm logon and architect of the Shanghai Museum of Glass, compares the current wave of museum construction to a previous push to build stadiums in China. That initiative faded soon after the Beijing Olympics, and the same fate, he predicts, will befall museums. "I can tell you," Krueger says, "in five years' time, no one will be building museums anymore."[16] This may be true. But whether or not it is, people will look back at the museums of the early twenty-first century as symbols of a significant architectural moment in China and the world.

* * *

Museums in China have a rather short history. The country's first museum, Shanghai's Siccawei Museum, was initiated by a Frenchman in 1868, and Nantong Museum, the first developed by a Chinese patron, opened in 1905. The first national museum, the National Historical Museum in Beijing, opened in 1912.[17] State-run museums now dominate the PRC, but the number of private museums is growing. According to *Jing Daily*, one reason for this growth is that China's megarich are investing in art as an alternative to the uncertain real estate market.[18] The *Huffington Post* lists another reason for funding art museums: wealthy Chinese are exhibiting a growing interest in philanthropy.[19] In building private museums, they may also aspire to be the Chinese version of Solomon R. Guggenheim or J. Paul Getty.

Distinctions between "state-run" and "private" are not as strict as their names imply. Public institutions have been known to show privately financed exhibitions. Philip Tinari, director of Beijing's Ullens Center for Contemporary Art, notes that the National Museum of China held an exhibition titled *Louis Vuitton, Voyages*, which he describes as "basically a trunk show."[20] Private museums necessarily exist on state-owned land (and adhere to state-mandated restrictions). Tinari says that, for a developer, building a private museum can be "a good pretext to get more land than you might otherwise get in China."

Despite these overlaps, public and private museums have different architectural expressions, according to Hua Li, principal of Trace Architecture Office and designer of the privately funded Museum of Handcraft Paper. "State-owned museums typically are more interested in form and trying to build a new image for a city as a cultural icon for urbanization," he says. "Private museums are more diversified, more specific."[21] Ma Yansong, principal of MAD Architects, talks about image building at the state-run Ordos Museum: "I think their main challenge was how they could build a museum to have a local cultural reference—it's Ordos Museum, not another museum."[22]

Zhao Qie, director of the Times Museum in Guangzhou, says the two different models can affect museums' curation as well. "State-run museums, of course, have stable funding and resources, and they might have the best location in the city," he says. "But there are restrictions; they usually don't have much freedom in their programming. In China a lot of state-run museums don't really have self-initiated exhibitions. As a privately funded museum, we have respectability; we have freedom and independence. We may have more niche and unique positioning."[23] Writer Kevin Holden Platt puts it more bluntly: "Many state-run cultural centers have declined to exhibit experimental Chinese art since its inception in the 1980s, and artists who reflect irreverently on China's communist past have been subject to state censure. Conversely, private galleries and museums that have emerged since the turn of the century have provided scattered sanctuaries for contemporary artworks."[24]

Curation is not always a consideration for architects of new museums, as the buildings do not always have predetermined collections. Shi Wenchian, project manager at MVRDV for the China Comic and Animation Museum, talks about the brief for some Chinese museums. "As architects you are to design the space according to the program and to the collection," she says. "You ask, 'What am I going to put there?' Often you get an answer saying, 'I don't know. First let's have a space, and keep the space flexible, then we'll see what we can put inside.'"[25]

Tinari says building museums without collections has precedent in China. "There are two different words for 'museum' in Chinese: *meishuguan*, which is an art museum, and *bowuguan*, a culture and artifacts museum. The first could be better translated as 'Kunsthalle,' an exhibition-driven institution for the fine arts. So in that way it's maybe not so surprising when art museums open without huge collections."[26] Liu Yingjiu, deputy director at Shanghai's Rockbund Art Museum, explains, "Especially after the 1950s, *meishuguan* became only a site for exhibitions—just a venue. It's not an institution based on a collection, research, scholarship, and curatorial experiments."[27] This is not a universal statement; Liu says that since the 1980s people have begun to rethink the museum's role. But, he says, "For many people, even now, the fine art museum is an exhibition hall where people can pay to show their works or the government can order a show of their own interests."

Some architects see benefits to designing a museum without a given collection. Mark Randel of David Chipperfield Architects says of the abbreviated brief for the Liangzhu Museum, "It was a nice opportunity to make a sculptural piece of architecture."[28] Fan Ling discusses the open plan of FANStudio's T Art Museum in Changsha: "It becomes a kind of embryo to cultivate the art, instead of trying to put all the art in place."[29] Others suggest that their museum's design might in fact affect its contents. Loretta Law of Foster + Partners talks about how multimedia art might work in the large gallery of the Datong Art Museum: "The scale of the space could actually contribute to how artists respond to the space."[30] Hu Qian says artists have had changing reactions to an irregularly shaped gallery in Arata Isozaki & Associates' CAFA Art Museum. "Before, artists said they were afraid of this kind of space," she says. "Now they all want this area for their exhibitions. This museum, they say, is a good fit for their project, or they want to make a piece that fits this space."[31]

Larys Frogier, director of the Rockbund Art Museum, agrees that the design decisions architects make for museums can affect artists' work. His own art deco–era building, he acknowledges, gives certain constraints to artists. But, he says, architects' current critique of the white cube of traditional museums and their attempts to transform the vision of modernist architecture bring new challenges. "There's a very strong energy now that comes from this," he says, "but it's not always easy to deal with." He adds, "Architects are bringing new ways, like a lot of curves, a lot of glass. And so sometimes the artist has to imagine how works can be in this kind of architecture. The artist could criticize the building, and in so doing could produce a creative project. But you can never be neutral in this kind of museum."[32]

* * *

Many times it is exactly those dynamic curves and walls of glass that make new museums so compelling. But noteworthy architecture, of course, does not guarantee a successful museum. The fact that visiting museums is not yet a common practice in China is one hindrance to their success. The government has tried to encourage visitation by offering free entry. According to *People's Daily*, "China introduced a policy of free admission to public museums [in 2009], and nearly 80 percent of the country's cultural and antique museums are now open to the public free of charge."[33] There are conflicting reports as to whether this initiative has had a positive effect on attendance.[34]

Architects interviewed for this book name other impediments to the success of new museums in China. Displaying exhibitions may be secondary to other purposes, such as providing meet-and-greet places for government officials or rental halls for company gatherings. Museums may lack directors and curators. They may be half full or even completely empty. (One should acknowledge that New York's Metropolitan Museum of Art opened at its original building before it acquired its first piece of art.[35] But it is unlikely that many of China's new museums will follow the Met's lead and become world-class venues.)

With all this in mind, it could be argued that the buildings in this collection are museums in name only. But who is to say that the museum model that Westerners know and love is the right model, or the only model? At a 2012 museum symposium, Philip Dodd, chair of London-based consultancy Made in China, questioned new museums that copy Western precedents for architecture, curation, and audience development: "The danger is that China will build museums that follow models of the twentieth century."[36] He said that Chinese examples that blur public and private designations and that are open to commercial funding might suggest a more viable future for museums everywhere. At the same symposium, curator and critic Hou Hanru questioned the permanent nature of the museum, stating that if a shop can change in five years, why not a museum?[37]

I cannot predict the future of museums. But I will say—with some hesitation—that new museum buildings in China might have great worth in and of themselves, regardless of what they contain. They may be comparable to churches in the United States. While some have lost their original purpose as houses of worship, they retain their prominence within their neighborhoods as communal halls, place makers, gathering points, and sources of local pride. They remain beloved in part because of their noteworthy design and construction. The same is true for many movie theaters, bank halls, and armories. A building type that holds the cultural and architectural aspirations of a nation at a particular moment in time is bound to be wrought with a certain gravitas. New museums in China have that weight. Within the sea of anonymous buildings that make up the contemporary urban fabric, they provide points of excellence. And as buildings dedicated to culture, they offer great potential for China's future artistic exploration, in whatever form it takes.

For consistency's sake, names of Chinese people are given with the family name before the personal name. I have made exceptions for a small number of Chinese names such as I. M. Pei, Yung Ho Chang, and Pei Zhu, which are popularly written in Western media with the personal name before the family name. Japanese names follow Western ordering, thus "Arata Isozaki" instead of "Isozaki Arata." This system may seem confusing, but it is the best I could devise given several imperfect options.

Locations for museums in this book are designated by city followed by province or autonomous region. Exceptions to this include the four municipalities—Beijing, Tianjin, Shanghai, and Chongqing—that are directly controlled by China's central government and therefore not under provincial or regional jurisdiction, as well as Hong Kong and Macao, which are special administrative regions of China and, again, not under provincial or regional jurisdiction. In these cases locations are listed by city alone. The date given for each project is the year of the building's completion or, for projects still under construction, the expected year of completion.

Quotes have been transcribed from interviews with the author, as indicated in the endnotes. I have been liberal with quotes when the speaker's first language is not English.

This is not meant to be a guidebook. As discussed in the introduction, museums in China often function differently from those in the West. They may not have regular exhibitions or visiting hours. In addition, some buildings originally designed as museums may no longer be used as such.

Jade Museum, Archi-
Union Architects,
Shanghai, 2013

NOTE TO THE READER

Harbin's China Wood Sculpture Museum follows the pattern of many new museums in China. A city develops a new area outside its historic core. A master plan is drawn up and roads are laid out. High-rise residences and high-priced commercial ventures move in. Soon the area is thriving. "Then they realize they need a cultural building," says Ma Yansong, principal of MAD Architects.[1]

Actually, Harbin needed a couple of cultural buildings: a museum for a collection of wood sculptures and another for paintings of snow- and ice-covered landscapes, familiar scenes in the northeastern city. "I convinced them to make one building," says Ma. "The reason I wanted to combine the two museums is: first, it's more convenient for people to see both together; second, I wanted this scale."

The site designated for construction had a unique proportion: 656 feet long and very thin. Ma saw an opportunity in this. He explains, "This city is being built piece by piece. Everyone is doing his own thing. So here I thought we should make one long building. With all these new residential towers behind it, it looks out of place. At the same time, it has a really dramatic relationship with the site."

The museum could almost be mistaken for a residential tower fallen on its side. But the details of neighboring towers—doors and windows and recesses—are nearly absent from the China Wood Sculpture Museum. The single long, twisted volume has an almost unbroken shell. Its few openings appear to be sized to the scale of the form rather than to human scale. The tube is covered in stainless-steel panels, "the same as the Disney Concert Hall," notes Ma. "The material has to work with the scale," he says. "The building is really long, and the lines on it are moving. When people pass by in a car, it feels like this building is there and also not there." Having few openings in the metal helps with the disappearing act.

MAD worked with computer modelers and fabricators to rationalize the facade design. By limiting the number of different steel panels, they could make the material economically feasible. "Then we had to fight with everyone," jokes Ma. He says that projects like this are built for political reasons, resulting in tight schedules tied to the term lengths of the politicians who commission the buildings. "The job of the construction team is to finish on time. So they think their work is perfect, but it's still so rough," says Ma. "For a lot of our buildings in China, we have this struggle. We have to do much more than architects should do to make our design happen. I see that as part of the experiment of this practice."

The museum's light, shiny facing; its long, curved form; and its location in a city best known for the annual Harbin International Ice and Snow Sculpture Festival cannot help but suggest an icicle. Ma claims otherwise. "We wanted to make the shape feel like something in between solid and liquid, between ice and water," he says. "It's a fluid, but it's not really, really soft. It has some shape."

Exhibition rooms are carved into this semisolid mass, and skylights and sidelights bring in shafts of low northern sunlight. One half of the museum has two stories for wood sculptures, and the other half, three stories for landscape paintings.

MAD's sculptural design won over Harbin's review board. "They really liked the model of the building," says Ma. But the stainless-steel facing did not get unanimous approval. One juror suggested the building be covered in wood, perhaps to acknowledge the wood sculptures that give the museum its name. "I said, 'No, of course not. It's important for the material to have a lightness,'" explains Ma. He later found out that this juror was Harbin's mayor. It seems he was not too offended by Ma's curt response. "I think he liked professionals to be professional," says Ma. "I think he respected that." The mayor gave his blessing to the stainless steel. And he later hired MAD to design an opera house, the next building slated to bring culture to Harbin.

TOP:
View toward
entrance

———

BOTTOM:
Detail of stainless-
steel panels on
facade

TOP:
View from
park to front of
museum during
construction

CENTER:
Rendering of
view toward main
entrance

BOTTOM:
Rendering of view
of side lighting at
north end

OPPOSITE

TOP:
Site plan

BOTTOM:
Diagram showing
circulation,
programming,
and lighting

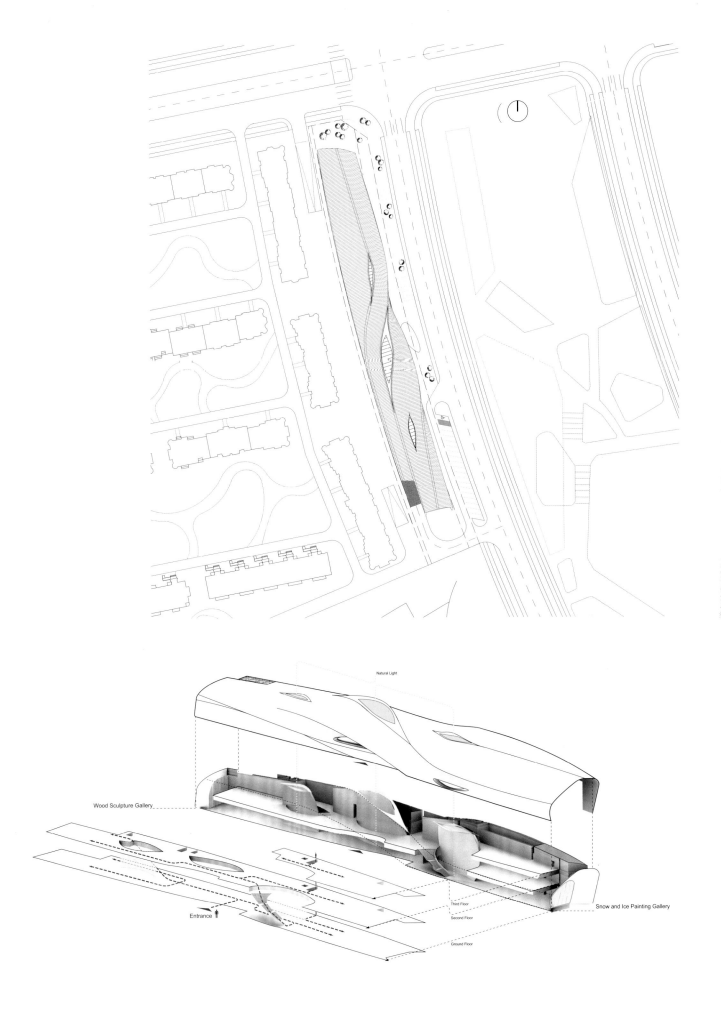

Natural Light

Wood Sculpture Gallery

Third Floor

Second Floor

Snow and Ice Painting Gallery

Ground Floor

Entrance

Architecture often responds to its site. But what happens when there's no *there* there? Such is the case of the Museum of Culture, Fine Arts, and Science, located outside Changchun city proper on an unremarkable site free of any distinctive context. "There was nothing. There was no identity for the place," says Nikolaus Goetze, partner of Architekten von Gerkan, Marg und Partner (GMP). "We decided we had to create our own identity."[2]

GMP chose not to produce a single monumental building. Instead, it composed a "museum town" of three smaller structures, one for each program. "They are like abstract, cubist-type buildings that were dropped down from the sky on a moonlike landscape," explains Goetze. The subtle ensemble has three white cubes that windmill around a central atrium. "We were a little bit tired of the designs of many museums in Asia, which always have to be the nicest and the craziest," he says. "We wanted to make a museum where the art is number one and the architecture is number two. The architecture has to serve the art."

The exteriors of the three structures share a similar aesthetic, materials, and perimeter, with minor differences in height and fenestration, as if the three were triplets wearing slightly different dresses so visitors can tell them apart. Greater differences occur inside, most notably in the atria. "The science museum has a very rectangular atrium, while the cultural museum has a canyon-like typology, and the fine arts museum has a diagonal shape," says Goetze. These variations help visitors find their way from the central atrium to the collection of their choice.

The Museum of Culture, Fine Arts, and Science is not, however, completely internalized. "Every building is a result of its genius loci," observes Goetze. The museum necessarily addresses site considerations, notably the area's long winters. "Changchun is a very rough northern Chinese city dominated by the cold, the snow, and the dry air." GMP used Chinese white granite to withstand the hard winter and limited the fenestration to keep the cold out. "These three cubes, with their roughness and composition and facade, never could be realized in Shenzhen," says Goetze. The forms are a better match for Changchun's mentality. He explains, "Changchun is not a very rich city; it's not like Shanghai. Therefore, we tried to minimize very complicated building technologies."

That this design approach bested less subtle entries in a 2006 competition for the museum may seem surprising. But not to Goetze. "Judges at this moment in China like rational architecture," he says. "They know you cannot build ten icon buildings in one town." He adds, "You must know that Changchun is dominated by Audi," whose partner, First Automobile Works, is the oldest and largest automotive company in China.[3] "The city may be used to the German way of thinking."

Central lobby
of Museum of
Science

MUSEUM OF CULTURE, FINE ARTS, AND SCIENCE

ARCHITEKTEN VON GERKAN, MARG UND PARTNER | CHANGCHUN, JILIN, 2011

TOP:
Stairs to central
entrance atrium

CENTER LEFT:
View from
southwest

CENTER RIGHT:
Detail of glazing

BOTTOM:
Lancet windows
in the Museum of
Fine Arts

OPPOSITE

TOP:
Worm's-eye view
inside Museum of
Science

BOTTOM:
First floor plan of,
clockwise from
left, museums of
culture, fine arts,
and science

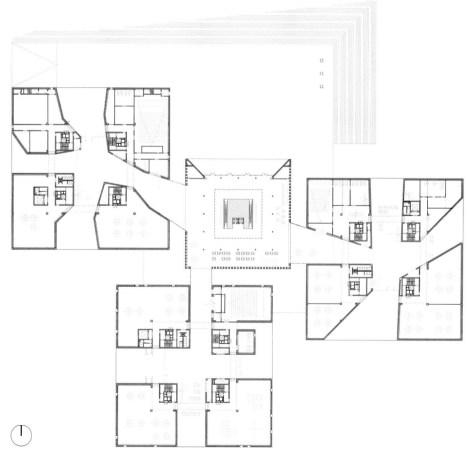

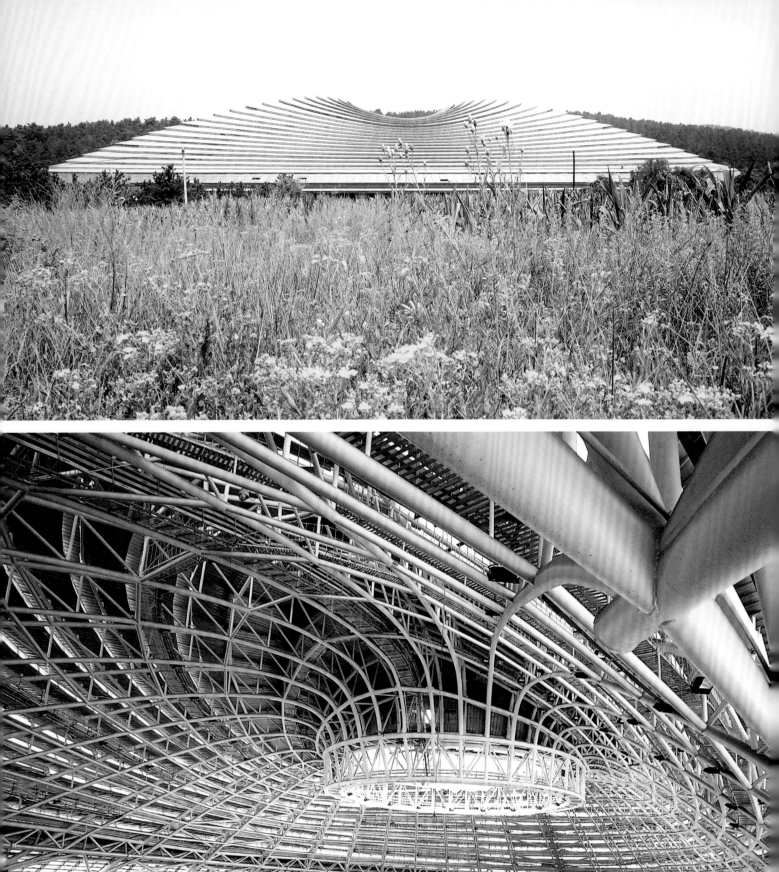

NIUHELIANG ARCHAEOLOGICAL MUSEUM

SUTHERLAND HUSSEY ARCHITECTS WITH PANSOLUTION INTERNATIONAL DESIGN

CHAOYANG, LIAONING, 2012

Tucked into the rugged mountains of Liaoning Province are a number of significant centers of ancient civilizations. One such place is Niuheliang, whose sixteen burial mounds and ritual centers are products of the Hongshan culture (4700–2900 BCE).[4] Since the 1980s archaeologists have been uncovering the area's artifacts, which include a pyramid-shaped burial mound, a female-spirit temple, and larger-than-life clay figures. The site is applying for inclusion on the UNESCO World Heritage List.[5] In the meantime, local officials are trying to preserve its treasures from the threat of optimistic grave robbers looking for as-yet-unearthed riches.

The Niuheliang Archaeological Museum, designed by Edinburgh-based Sutherland Hussey Architects with Beijing-based Pansolution International Design, covers Niuheliang's Site Two. "One of the biggest challenges was the fact that we couldn't put any structure into the site," says Charlie Sutherland, director of Sutherland Hussey Architects.[6] At roughly 650 by 250 feet, Site Two is the largest gathering of tombs in the area. It required a lot of protection.

To span the vast site, the architects designed a large shell for the museum. Its tough exterior not only constitutes a defense against potential thieves but also protects the fragile excavation from the hot and cold extremes of Liaoning weather. Sutherland compares the dome's structural system to a bicycle wheel, with spoke-like trusses leading from an elliptical base to a central compression ring that hovers directly above a circular tomb, the main tomb of Site Two.

The museum's shell is covered in oxidized, prepatinated copper with ribbon-thin bands of glazing. The metal is no stranger to Niuheliang; a copper earring was found in one of its Neolithic tombs.[7] Sutherland says that the copper's green color and the museum's elliptical form were inspired by a jade object found on-site. Hongshan culture is known for the jade buried with its dead, and the area's jade artifacts include coiled dragons and a turtle.[8] Sutherland notes another inspiration for the museum: "the local landscape, this kind of rolling land form."

Inside the museum, the hole in the roof is the centerpiece for visitors who choose to look up rather than down. Its glazed oculus offers dramatic lighting, and its truss-gathering compression ring makes a strong sculptural statement. The oculus, like the tombs, can be experienced only from afar. Visitors walk along the museum's perimeter on an elevated gallery. From there, a pedestrian bridge connects to the landscape beyond the shell, where jade hunters can roam the mountains of Liaoning uninhibited.

TOP:
Exterior view

BOTTOM:
View of oculus and compression ring at center of interior

TOP:
View of museum
within rugged
mountains of
Liaoning Province

———

CENTER:
Interior view

———

BOTTOM:
Uncovered
archaeological
Site Two

OPPOSITE

TOP:
Typical plan

———

CENTER:
Long section

———

BOTTOM:
Axonometric

10

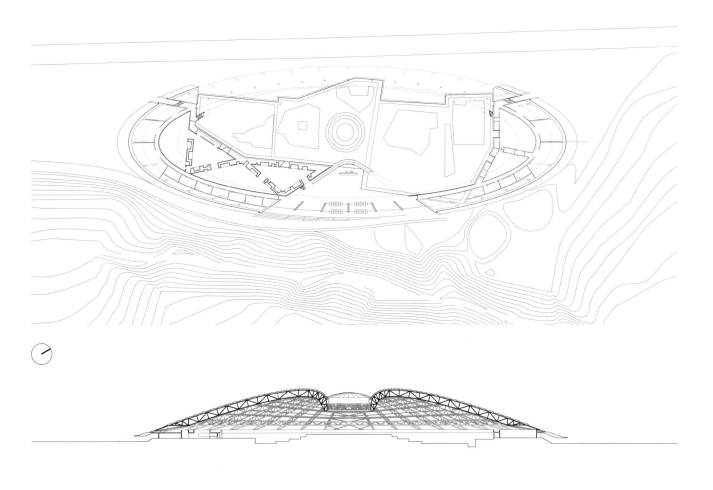

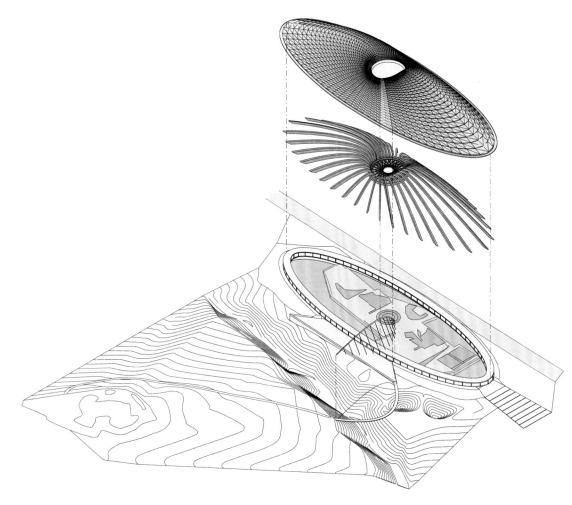

The Qinhuangdao Bird Museum nestles into its beachside site. Its long, rectangular forms gather head to tail, as if snuggling for warmth and protection. "Chairman Mao composed a poem about this site, about the boats anchoring on the shore," says Yu Kongjian, principal of Turenscape. "The building was inspired by this image."[9] Like these boats, the museum finds strength in numbers as its components huddle against the forces of nature. And like the boats, "the building tries to catch the breeze and the view," says Yu.

Until recently, there was not much of a view to catch. Misuse and mismanagement, Yu explains, had made the beach anything but idyllic. An unsightly concrete embankment stood out in the water, and remnants of an amusement park dotted the shore with architectural debris. Turenscape's Qinhuangdao Beach Restoration project transformed the litter-strewn, four-mile-long beach that extends from the museum. The American Society of Landscape Architects referred to the design as "ecological surgery."[10] The work included protecting the beach from erosion, recovering the wetlands, constructing small islands for bird sanctuaries, replacing the concrete embankment with a more ecologically minded riprap, and building the Qinhuangdao Bird Museum to educate visitors about the site.

The museum sits in a wetland in a shallow tributary area, just south of where the Xinhe River empties into the Bohai Sea. It is in an important bird migration corridor, and the designers have made the birds part of the museum's exhibit. Yu recalls the design discussion: "There's a bird sanctuary nearby; why don't we just let nature tell the story?" Turenscape gave visitors many ways to access the views. The museum has two entrances, one into a glass-faced lobby and another onto a rooftop where visitors can look out over the wetland. The building boxes open onto the site through picture windows that take up almost the entire surface of their waterside facades. Even some of the floors are used for viewing. Through the bottoms of the eastern elevated boxes, visitors can see bird-nesting sites below. Those who want an even closer view can walk out into the wetland on platforms that extend from the building.

Turenscape recognized that the museum would become not only a place to take in the view but also itself an object in the landscape. The museum shows two faces: a concrete face to the road and a wooden face to the water. "The concrete part is more a dialogue with the city," says Yu. "Its white facade allows people to read the museum's sculptural form." Turenscape set the concrete with subtle patterns that suggest seaweed to make the concrete look more like natural rock. "The wood facade is more related to nature, and it opens up into nature," says Yu. From the water, one might just see the suggestion of Chairman Mao's little wooden boats in the building.

Entrance to viewing deck at center, with entrance to museum at right

OPPOSITE

TOP:
Rendering
of the
Qinhuangdao
Beach
Restoration
project with
island bird
sanctuaries at
left and the
Qinhuangdao
Bird Museum
at right

TOP:
Facade facing
water

CENTER:
Sections

BOTTOM:
Facade facing city

BOTTOM:
Plan

NORTHEAST AND NORTH   14

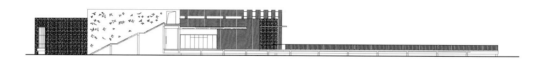

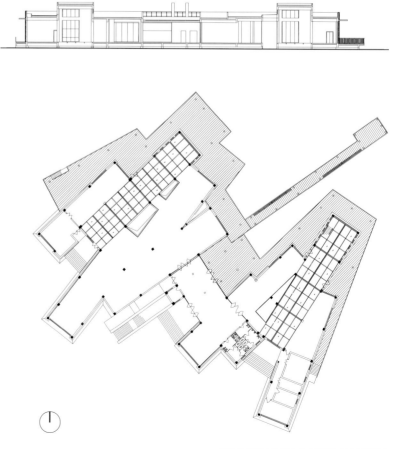

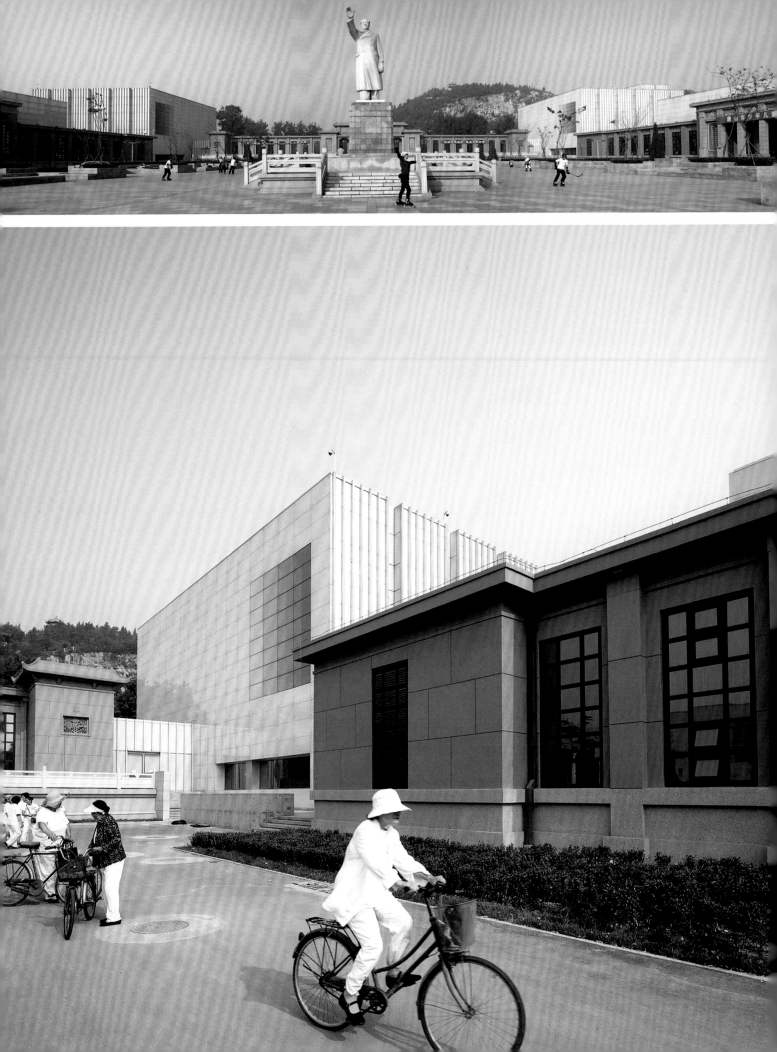

Tangshan Museum sits at the heart of the historic city, with Phoenix Mountain Park at its back. The museum reuses three buildings constructed in 1968, during the Cultural Revolution. Wang Hui, principal of Urbanus Architecture & Design, says the structures are precious to the local community, not for their architecture but for their history. They are the only large public buildings that withstood Tangshan's devastating 1976 earthquake. Wang says the goal of Urbanus's design for the Tangshan Museum was to "elevate the memory of the city as well as bring new facilities" to the site.[11]

"Our addition is actually quite minimal," says Wang. Urbanus retained the facades of the extant buildings, including the Maoist sayings inscribed at their entrances. It inserted skylights to bring light into the gallery spaces. It tucked two new buildings—one used for exhibitions, the other for a cafe and shop—into corner spaces between the buildings. The additions allow the previously disconnected parts to become one continuous 431,000-square-foot, U-shaped whole.

Viewed from the site's central plaza, the relatively low new buildings blend in with the 1968 structures. "You won't notice that there's a big change," says Wang. Urbanus made sure that the additions did not interfere with the view from the plaza to Phoenix Mountain. It faced the additions in white textured glass in order to diminish their presence next to the older concrete buildings. Viewed from the back of the site, where the additions are not hidden behind the originals, the glass gives the museum a high-tech appearance. "We wanted to use the most advanced material to show that the city is in the process of entering into a contemporary life," explains Wang.

Urbanus's subtle intervention is a product of both budget and intention. "Tangshan is a second-tier or third-tier city, unlike Shanghai or Beijing, where you see all those crazy, amazing things," says Wang. He hopes that with this minimal design Urbanus has created a place that works well for both official government events and the everyday enjoyment of Tangshan residents.

To that end, Wang points out the museum's many indoor public spaces and its free admission. "The exhibition spaces tend to be less important now," he says, "and this series of 'public living rooms' within the space, free to everyone, becomes a more important feature." To increase the use of the existing outdoor plaza, Urbanus added "urban sofas." These stepped designs allow for small gatherings to coexist with the dancers and in-line skaters who frequent the plaza.

"Right now the outdoor plaza is much better used than the indoor spaces," says Wang, explaining that many people are too intimidated to enter the museum. The state-published *People's Daily* noted the national problem of low museum attendance in an article titled "Free Entry Cannot Attract Visitors for Chinese Museums."[12] "Comparatively, this is still a high-culture facility for the public," says Wang. "It will take time to educate people about how to use it and to make it an extension of their own living space."

TOP:
View from plaza toward Phoenix Mountain

BOTTOM:
View showing addition at left and renovation at right

OPPOSITE

TOP:
View from plaza
at night
—
CENTER:
View of "urban
sofas" in plaza
—
BOTTOM:
Interior of addition

TOP:
Sections and east
elevation
—
BOTTOM LEFT:
Site plan
—
BOTTOM RIGHT:
First floor plan

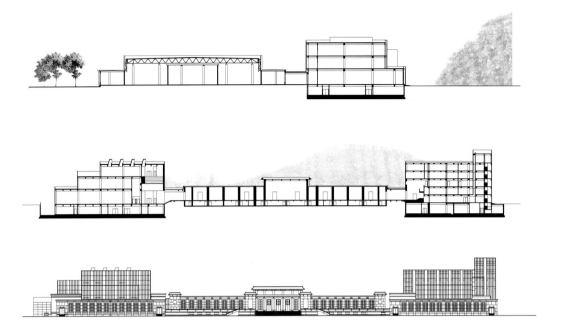

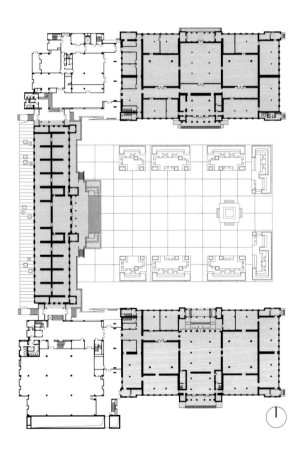

Architect Shin Takamatsu is known for the mechanical imagery of such buildings as Origin I (1981) and Ark (1983), both in Kyoto, Japan.[13] Their parts seem to be diecast rather than constructed with standard building materials. The buildings are very much of their time and of their place.

For the Tianjin Museum, his first building in China, Takamatsu decided to use natural rather than mechanical references. "When I visited the site, it was quite vast and had no special features," he says.[14] The site area is 540,000 square feet, and the coastal megalopolis of Tianjin circa 2001 was not, it seems, a source of design inspiration. "I was at a loss as to how to find a context—a clue to the design," he continues. "At that time, I saw white birds flying in the contaminated and mud-colored sky that was typical in Tianjin. This appealing sight gave me the direct source of my creation's inspiration."

The flying birds took on a very literal form. "I came to think of the white bird as a swan and made a concrete image of a swan laying itself down," says Takamatsu. The swan, with wings extended as if in flight, was abstracted into a strict circular plan and a low, arched elevation. The museum's landscape design attempted to create a new context in Tianjin's Yinhe Park rather than to respond to the existing urban condition. "It was meant to create a quiet, new scenery," explains Takamatsu. The landscape continued the avian metaphor, as the swan's neck is represented by a bridge over an artificial pond.

This swan is an especially big bird. With a total area of 365,000 square feet over three floors, the museum was the largest in China when it was completed in 2004. To contend with the scale, Takamatsu worked with the engineer Mamoru Kawaguchi on the submission to the Tianjin Museum's 2001 international design competition and on executing the design. Kawaguchi & Engineers' work elsewhere includes cable systems and membrane structures, but here the designers developed a simple hybrid structure made of steel and reinforced concrete with a metal roof.[15] Takamatsu explains, "As a result of our research into construction technology in China in those days, we decided to use no special technique." Construction technology has changed since 2001, and new Chinese museums have surpassed the Tianjin Museum in size. But Takamatsu's swan remains a unique and forceful statement in the city

Night views of museum and bridge

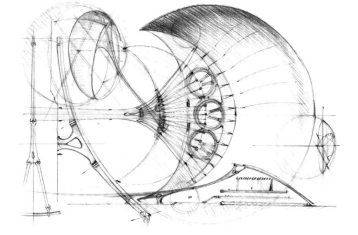

TOP:
Bird's-eye view

CENTER:
Views of interior

BOTTOM:
Concept sketch

OPPOSITE

TOP:
Second floor plan

BOTTOM:
Sections

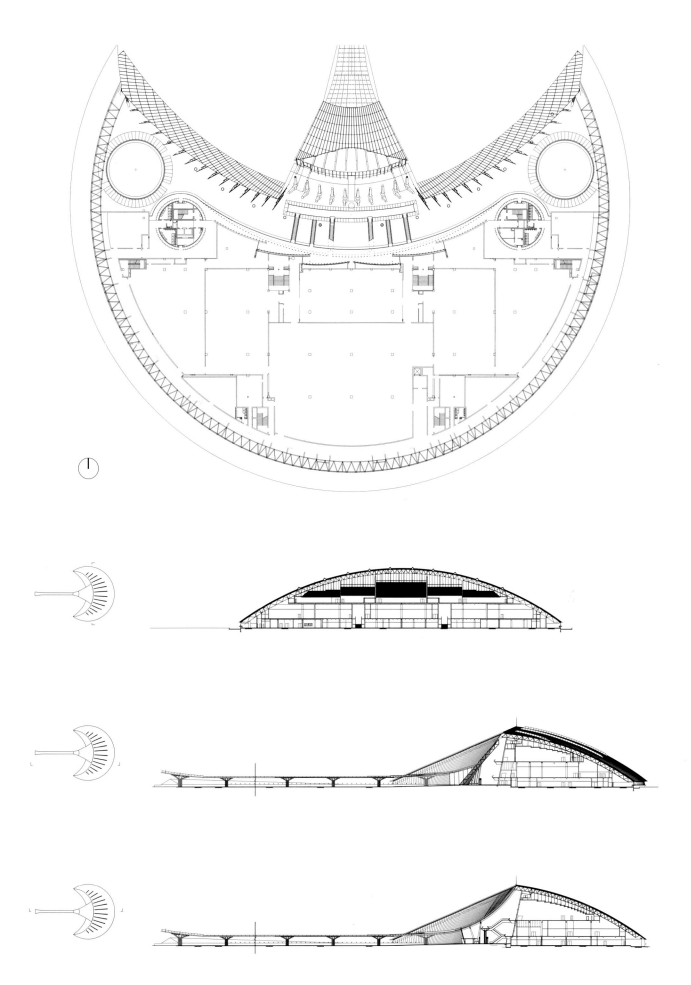

Arata Isozaki's art museum for the China Central Academy of Fine Arts is a warm, rounded shell hiding an active, skylit interior. Its design, materials, composition, siting—its entire architecture—seem complete, the work of an artist who has mastered his media. One can see influences of Isozaki's earlier projects in the design. But the CAFA Art Museum is not a pastiche of the architect's fifty years of practice. For this, his first work in Beijing and his first museum in China, Isozaki took a studied approach. "CAFA is a fine-arts university, and its professors have very strong ideas about exhibitions and museums," says Hu Qian, partner of Isozaki + HuQian Partners, an associated office of Arata Isozaki & Associates that oversaw the project. "We needed to make a lot of studies to convince them and make them feel good."[16]

CAFA, China's "only art academy of higher learning directly under the Ministry of Education," was founded in 1950, and its roots date back to 1918. It has six schools and colleges, including a school of architecture.[17] Isozaki's on-campus museum for the academy replaces a 1953 building in central Beijing.[18] The design houses a wide range of work, including CAFA's historic collection as well as contemporary and student exhibitions. To address all these complexities, the design team prepared fifty to sixty architectural schemes, according to Hu. "How to divide the small spaces from the large spaces is important here," she says. "It's not like older museum models—a huge space with some partitions inside to separate the room. For this project we have large rooms that can allow installation artists to make site-specific work." Typically, museum walls simply try to stay out of the way of this kind of art. "But in the CAFA Art Museum, we tried to make a background that can inspire artists and influence their projects." Hu adds, "We also included some more traditional spaces for oil paintings and the like."

First floor lobby

A central ramp joins the big and small gallery spaces. "Isozaki-san has a lot of ramps in his museums," says Hu. And he has a lot of museums in his portfolio, including the Museum of Modern Art in Gunma (1974), the Kitakyushu City Museum of Art in Fukuoka (1974), and the Museum of Contemporary Art in Los Angeles (1986).[19] "Here we're trying to use the ramp not just for circulation but also as a part of the exhibition. For example, at the entrance hall, many exhibitions hang from the ceiling. So when you walk along the ramp, you can see all the parts of the exhibition and also experience the space." An additional ramp is included on the exterior, "not for design but for function," Hu says. It allows access to a sunken garden on the museum's very tight site.

The architects fit a big program into the small site by building two floors below ground and four above. A window from the sunken garden brings light into the lower floors. Vertical windows at the main, staff, and service entrances yield more light. Natural light comes from above as well, through glass skylights with glass-fiber membranes underneath to soften the rays. Hu compares these skylights to those at Isozaki's museum in Gunma. They bring diffused light to public spaces and to galleries earmarked for contemporary installations. Rooms with oil paintings and scrolls are lit with controlled artificial lighting.

The museum's small site also influenced its form. The L-shaped curve fits along a curved road and skirts an existing sculpture studio to avoid blocking the students' sunlight. Isozaki covered this form in slate, which fits in with the surrounding gray brick buildings. "On the campus, all the buildings are very square, rigid forms," says Hu. "Isozaki-san wanted to follow the existing context. Also, it was the client's requirement that we didn't make the museum too iconic. We had already chosen an organic form, different from the other buildings. But maybe in the facade and material our design could be similar to them." The designers initially considered facing the building in small tile, like that Isozaki had used in his Nara Centennial Hall (1998) in Japan. But the budget for CAFA did not allow it. Slate was less expensive and made possible the curved exterior that allows for the curved interior.

The tall, skylit spaces under the curved roof are features of the museum. "The main focus of this museum is the part for contemporary art," says Hu. "These galleries are a little different from the white cube, but not too iconic." Hu recalls a recent conversation about these galleries with the director of the CAFA Art Museum. "Before, artists said they were afraid of this kind of space," she says. "Now they all want this area for their exhibitions. This museum, they say, is a good fit for their project, or they want to make a piece that fits this space."

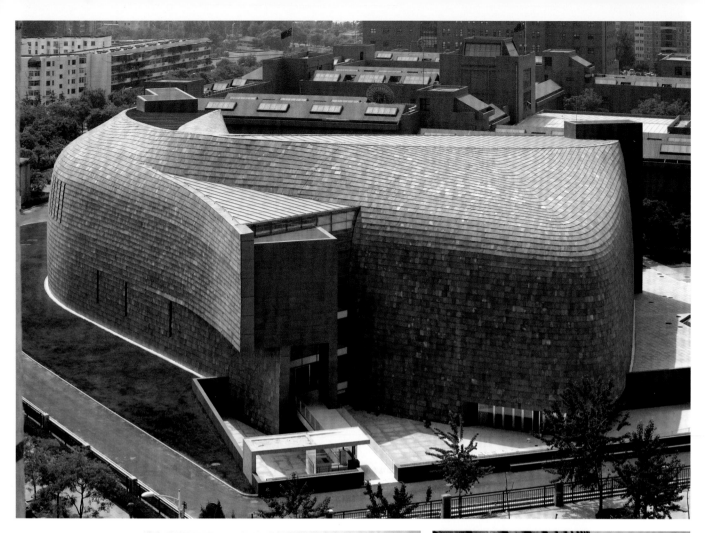

TOP AND BOTTOM
RIGHT:
Views under
skylight
———
BOTTOM LEFT:
View from
central ramp

OPPOSITE

TOP:
First floor plan
———
BOTTOM:
Roof plan

28

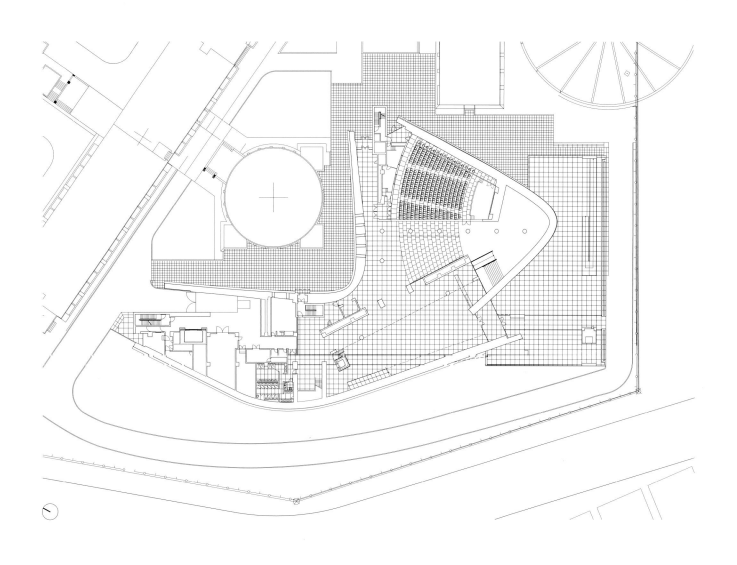

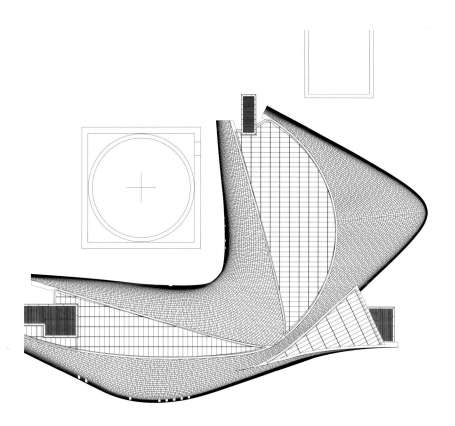

"If we talk about traditional Chinese architecture, we have to talk about roofs," says Stephan Schütz, partner of Architekten von Gerkan, Marg und Partner. "I think the roof is *the* element of traditional Chinese buildings, and that's why we selected it—to give symbolic meaning to this extension of the National Museum."[20] GMP's competition design for this museum on the east side of Tiananmen Square featured a large bronze roof floating above a courtyard. It could be used as a covered public square to offer visitors the protection from rain and sun that Tiananmen does not. The museum's main exhibition hall for Chinese history would sit inside the roof, elevated to a room with a significant view. "From this roof level you could see all the important historic architecture in Beijing: the Forbidden City, the Temple of Heaven," says Schütz. It was a big idea, and with it GMP won the design competition in 2004.

But after nearly a year of work on this design, the project suddenly was put on hold and went back for review. "I never got into a deep discussion about it," says Schütz, "but I heard that the Chinese architectural experts involved in this jury doubted a little bit these big and very radical ideas—for example, this roof." Local projects such as Herzog & de Meuron's Beijing National Stadium (nicknamed Bird's Nest by Beijingers), Paul Andreu's National Grand Theater (Giant Egg), and OMA's CCTV Headquarters (Big Boxer Shorts) were in varying stages of design and construction, and they were causing a stir. "They were talking a lot at that time about Western architects using China as a laboratory for their ideas," says Schütz. "Especially on Tiananmen Square, the Chinese wanted something more in balance with the buildings built in 1959." These 1959 buildings have great importance in Beijing. The National Museum of China, designed by Zhang Kaiji, and the Great Hall of the People, designed by Zhang Bo, face each other across the square.[21] They are two of Mao Zedong's Ten Great Buildings, constructed to commemorate the tenth anniversary of the founding of the People's Republic.

The client and GMP discussed a less radical separation between the old and new designs, to avoid overshadowing the historic building. "We thought this could be a way to deal with this building," says Schütz. "We know this from a lot of projects in Germany." He cites Munich's Alte Pinakothek by Hans Döllgast (1957) and Berlin's Neues Museum by David Chipperfield (2009) as examples of successful historical and contemporary cohabitation.[22] GMP went back to the drawing board to study

details of the extant building and to discuss Chinese architecture with local experts. Its new design took fragments from the original and abstracted them in a contemporary way. "Everybody who visits the building should feel that this part is from 1959 and the other part from 2011," says Schütz. The trained eye will see the differences between the Soviet-influenced Chinese architecture and the German contemporary interpretation of the same. The untrained eye might not.

GMP's new approach focused on another strategy from their competition design: linking the building's two parts. The National Museum of China combines the National Museum of the Chinese Revolution in its north wing and the National Museum of Chinese History in the south.[23] The north wing now holds an exhibition gallery, and the south, administration offices and a library. GMP linked these with one large hall. Its 850-foot length was a given, but Schütz offers another reason for its colossal size: "When people come from such a huge square, they expect something big when they enter the museum." This might explain the hall's 89-foot ceiling height. A grand central staircase and two smaller side staircases direct visitors from the hall up to the art. "As you come closer to the exhibition halls, the scale turns down to a human scale," says Schütz.

GMP relied on traditional models to compose the materials in the entrance hall. "All the classical public buildings in China—temples, palaces, but also some smaller-scale architecture—have stone bases with a wood structure above and then a coffered ceiling," says Schütz. These three elements are duplicated in the entrance hall. Smaller rooms use a different combination of materials: local granite, cherry wood, and dark steel. GMP kept a consistent color palette throughout more than two million square feet to create a sort of branding for the museum. There are a few exceptions to this: a red concert hall, a blue cinema, and a rooftop banquet hall with green recycled glass suggesting jade.

This skylit banquet hall joins smaller restaurants, reception rooms, and a visitors' terrace in GMP's revised roof. "We kept the idea of this floating roof," says Schütz, "but it doesn't contain any exhibitions right now." Instead of containing the main exhibition hall for Chinese history, the built roof accommodates invitation-only spaces. It is not as big as originally designed, but it does match the height of the Great Hall of the People across the square. "From Tiananmen Square you see that there is a new and bigger building standing within the courtyard," says Schütz, "but it's in the second row, so it doesn't show up so much." The roof is not the grand gesture GMP initially envisioned, but it may be just the right nod to its neighbors on the square.

View of entrance hall

TOP:
Tiananmen
Square, with the
National Museum
of China on
the left and the
Mausoleum of
Mao Zedong on
the right

—

BOTTOM LEFT:
Interior of west
entrance

BOTTOM RIGHT:
Entrance
doors made
of perforated
bronze plates
inspired by an
ancient bronze
panel in the
museum's
collection

OPPOSITE

TOP:
Space between
old and new
entrances on
west

—

BOTTOM:
West entrance
hall

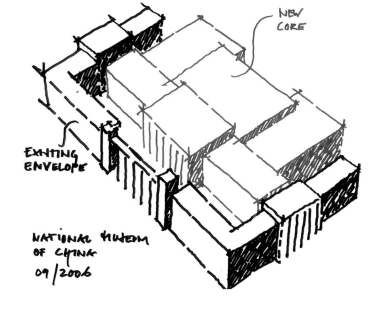

NEW CORE

EXISTING ENVELOPE

NATIONAL MUSEUM OF CHINA 09/2006

TOP LEFT:
Local granite
and cherry wood
cladding is used in
the building

TOP RIGHT:
View of upper-
level interior

BOTTOM LEFT:
Winning
competition
proposal

BOTTOM RIGHT:
Concept sketch of
revised design

OPPOSITE

TOP:
West elevation,
north elevation

CENTER:
Section

BOTTOM:
Basement
level plan with
cinema, theater,
library and
offices

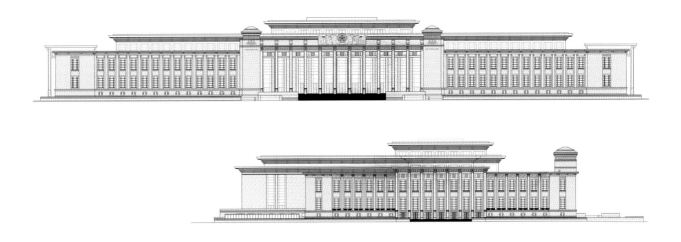

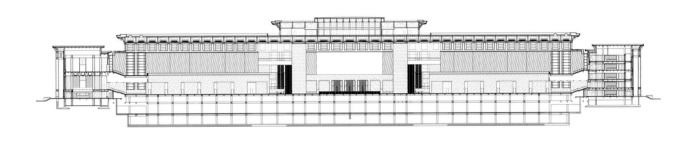

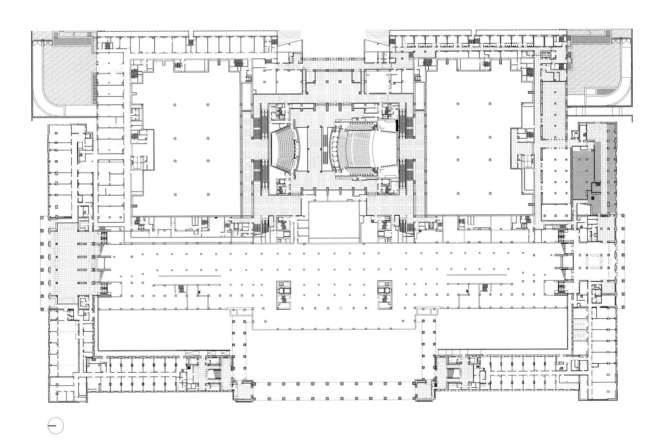

When we started to work on the Songzhuang Art Museum, we talked with [museum director] Li Xianting and the local artists to see what they thought about this art center as the community's first public building," says Xu Tiantian, principal of DnA Design and Architecture. "It could be quite monumental, because it would represent the history of Songzhuang and also the history of Chinese contemporary art. On the other hand, it was also like a temple for the community—an art temple."[24]

Xu describes the origins of the Songzhuang community at the center of the design. Artists who had been forced to leave their commune on the grounds of Beijing's Old Summer Palace came to the small village in the early 1990s. There, beyond Beijing's Sixth Ring Road, they could afford inexpensive homes and studios and work undisturbed. Early residents included Yue Minjun (known for his big-grinned self-portraits) and Fang Lijun (known for his Cynical Realism).[25] The success of these and other artists drew more and more people into a kind of "utopia of Chinese art," says Xu. "They started with only four or five artists, and now there must be over ten thousand."

Still, Songzhuang has not gone the way of Beijing's 798 Art Zone, where art spaces— and the coffee shops and souvenir stands that accompany them—have pushed out all the locals. Xu says, "In Songzhuang there's really a balance of local living and art." DnA wanted to acknowledge that balance in its design for the museum. "And so we all agreed that we would give it a large plaza, first of all, and the building would be quite a monument. But it would also reflect the local community."

Community involvement was central from the start. The construction team was from the village—men who had previously built only small houses and some light industrial facilities. This was their first museum. The construction used local materials: glass and floor tiles from Songzhuang and brick from a neighboring village. The concrete structure was faced with brick because "brick is kind of a memory, used out of respect for the local context," says Xu.

Village people continued interacting with the museum after it was built. Some serve as receptionists and security guards. Others make the museum their destination on after-dinner walks. "In their routine lives they see performance art, and there are always shows opening," says Xu. "So they're very educated in art." In addition, she says, villagers have entered the businesses of art framing, packaging, and transportation.

The design of the museum is a sectional idea. "The concept of the building is quite simple," says Xu. "We opened up the whole ground floor and then lifted up the major exhibition halls to the upper level." The thin strip of a glass-enclosed entrance level is used for the lobby and public facilities. "It's very transparent," says Xu. "You can wander around the outside or you can walk around inside. It's open for both the artists and the villagers." The high-ceilinged, brick-faced upper floor contains the art. Its solid red walls, unbroken by windows, put on a monumental face. This second story is made of four dissimilar boxes: one for an auditorium and three for variously sized exhibitions and artworks. One gallery is oversized. "The work of Chinese artists has become larger and larger. I don't know for what reason—everyone goes for big," laughs Xu.

Vertical voids cut between the exhibition boxes. They bring light into one of the second-floor gallery spaces and also the large first-floor space. "The ground floor is surrounded by glass," says Xu, "so light comes from the facade, but also from the central courtyard." A kind of inverted skylight, a glass floor below a beam used as a bench, physically connects museum and village. "When you're in the art space, these presentations can be kind of overwhelming," says Xu. "So you take a seat and start to realize what's in the real world. You see the plaza, the people walking by, to give you a break." At the same time, people on the plaza can look up into the gallery and "maybe see a bit of the work on the wall."

Some time has passed since DnA's ideas have taken form. Xu says she is happy with the current state of the Songzhuang Art Museum, "even though it might not be very similar to what we were expecting. When you think about a museum, it's always very institutional, very beautiful, a very quiet space, very well maintained—almost a luxury, taking you out of daily life. But this isn't." She says the museum is instead "just very real," maybe a more communal than monumental statement. "The staff of the museum is all local villagers, so they're chatting, they're sitting on a stool they've brought from home, they're knitting. The museum has taken on its own life, and maybe that's how it should be."

Exterior views showing glass-enclosed first floor and brick-clad exhibition halls

OPPOSITE

TOP:
View toward first
floor stairway

TOP:
Exterior view

BOTTOM
LEFT:
View toward first
floor stairway

BOTTOM
RIGHT:
View of courtyard

BOTTOM LEFT:
Window from
outside plaza
to second floor
gallery

BOTTOM RIGHT:
Window from
second floor
gallery to outside
plaza

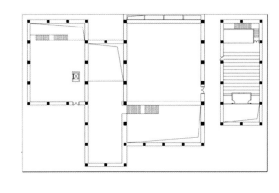

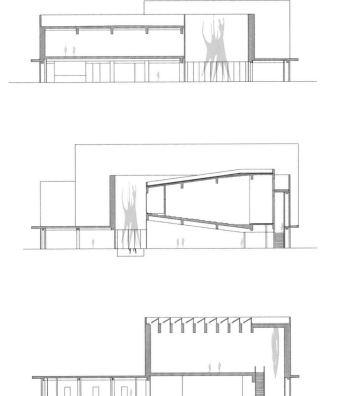

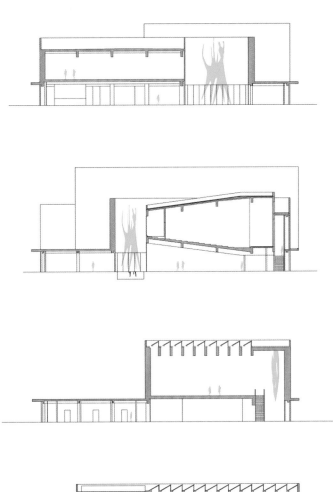

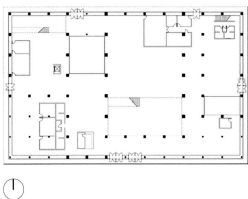

The urban planning museum is a must-have for Chinese cities. "Every self-respecting city is building one," says John van de Water, partner of Amsterdam- and Beijing-based NEXT Architects.[26] These museums celebrate their locales with exhibitions that tell "a large part about the past, hardly anything about what's going on now, and everything about the future," he says. The centerpiece of most is a large-scale model of the existing and future city. Those familiar with the 1964 Panorama of the City of New York will have a notion of this.[27]

Van de Water explains the genesis of such museums. "Mayors always have to show their progress in order to get promoted," he says. "The first thing they do is build an urban planning museum in order to display the CBDs [central business districts] they're going to build, the international exhibition center, the high-grade infrastructure, the new airport, and the new landmark TV tower." His Chaoyang Urban Planning Museum promotes a district rather than an entire city. But that district has more than its share to show off, including the Olympic Green from the 2008 Beijing Games, the 798 Art Zone, and Beijing's CBD, featuring the work of another Dutch firm, the CCTV Headquarters by OMA.

The museum is next to the Olympic beach-volleyball stadium in Chaoyang Park. It is on the site of the former Beijing Yanshan Gas Utensil Factory, a 1960s-era model factory. NEXT reused three existing factory buildings, filled the T-shaped space between them with flexible space (so flexible that it was once used for a Jean Paul Gaultier fashion show), and added glass- and aluminum-clad spaces on top.[28] Visitors take one of two routes through the museum. "It's always important to incorporate a VIP route in your public designs here," says van de Water, "because they always have to take shortcuts." General visitors follow a sixty-minute route, but VIPs spend only ten minutes in the museum, ending at a private club in the uppermost addition.

NEXT designed an undulating roof for the new areas, to contrast with the factories' historic texture. As van de Water recounts in his book, *You Can't Change China, China Changes You*, his colleague suggested promoting the form's connection to the traditional Chinese "lucky cloud." The cloud had been recently depicted on the Olympic torch. "I reacted with a smile: 'Dutch concepts are about conditions. Chinese concepts are about form,'" writes van de Water. "Without waiting for a reply, I continued: 'Let's make a lucky cloud building!'"[29] Both arguments helped win over the jury for the design competition.

Only nine months separated the start of the competition from an all-important opening for the mayor of London, who was visiting to gather information for the London Olympics. Then the museum had a second opening to reveal the CBD's second phase. "When the Urban Planning Museum unveiled an enormous 1:750 scale model of Beijing 2020," write Neville Mars and Adrian Hornsby, "residents flocked less to see what was new than to find out if their homes had been swallowed."[30]

View of interior
with undulating
roof

OPPOSITE

TOP:
Exterior view

———

CENTER:
Elevations

———

TOP AND BOTTOM
LEFT:
Exterior views

———

BOTTOM RIGHT:
Interior view

BOTTOM:
Routes for
general visitors
(left) and for VIP
visitors (right)

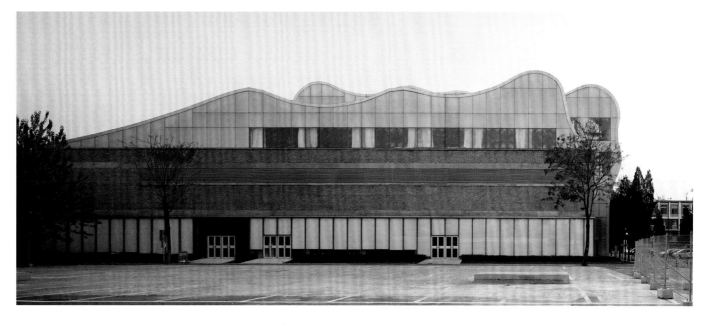

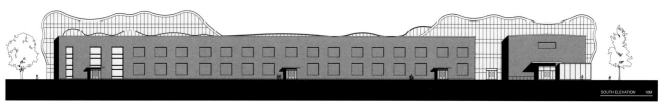

SOUTH ELEVATION 10M

WEST ELEVATION 10M

EAST ELEVATION 10M

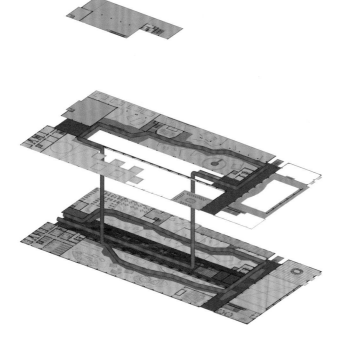

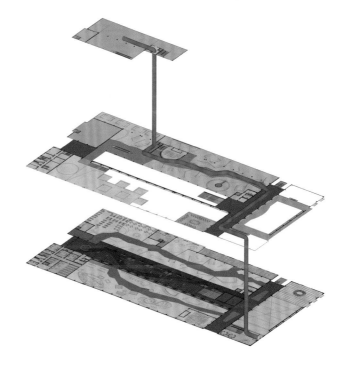

IBERIA CENTER FOR CONTEMPORARY ART

APPROACH ARCHITECTURE STUDIO | BEIJING, 2008

Beijing's 798 Art Zone is one of the city's most popular tourist destinations. The enclave of former electronics factories started emptying out in the 1980s. In the mid-1990s art students and professors moved into the low-rent spaces and set up homes and studios. Independent artists soon followed, and eventually 798 became an art mecca.[31] Today it is home to high-minded ventures like the Ullens Center for Contemporary Art, renovated by Jean-Michel Wilmotte and Ma Qingyun in 2007.[32] It also contains galleries where "art" might be better labeled "souvenir."

Liang Jingyu, principal of Approach Architecture Studio, recalls his early discussions with the sponsors of Iberia Center for Contemporary Art about setting up a venue in 798. "I was trying to make sure that they were making something bigger than a gallery," he says.[33] His client, a Chinese Spanish importer-exporter, who was interested in contemporary art, was just beginning to conceive the Iberia Center. "The architectural structure was basically happening before they had this institute," says Liang.

Approach Architecture and its client began exploring options for the space and its use. In this investigation, Liang was inspired by 798's factories. These industrial buildings, built in 1952 by East German architects, are now protected as "Exceptional Modern Architecture."[34] "We had this raw space," recalls Liang. "There were no white walls or marble floors. Why not make this a place to produce art? Not necessarily to collaborate with artists, but maybe with curators." The client was receptive to the idea of a malleable space—at first. "We found out that it's not that easy," says Liang. "The freedom was limited, and the budget was also limited if you want to redo your space every time you do a show." Instead of the planned "permanently unfinished site," the museum is a fixed building.

The design for Iberia Center connects three extant buildings. Except for the old structure and walls, and some Chinese characters written on the beams, everything is new. Liang mentions that many architects use recycled bricks in their projects at 798; the industrial aesthetic has become the image of the district. But he chose to renovate with all new materials to distinguish the old from the new.

These new materials include the bricks on the museum's front facade, a 164-foot wall linking the three buildings. A lower, curving section of bricks (which seems appropriate for a Spanish institution) swings out from the wall plane. Liang says the curve "is not necessarily an expression, but a solution"; it met the client's request for extra space at the front of the museum. Approach Architecture got around fitting the building within the property line by submitting roof plans instead of floor plans for approval. The curved base steps over the line a bit, but the roof falls within it, and so the design was accepted. The resulting space between the new curve and the old facade was originally used as a cafe serving Spanish cuisine. The cafe did not last. In an art district where restaurants and shops selling unadventurous fare threaten to outnumber studios and galleries showing experimental art, it seems this unconventional addition could not compete.

View toward entrance

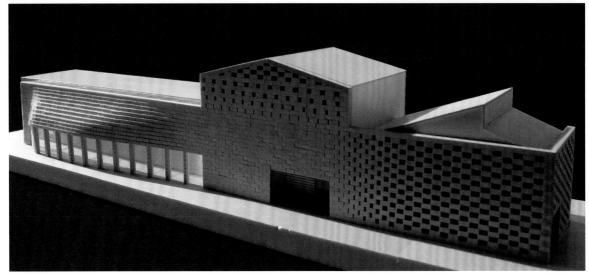

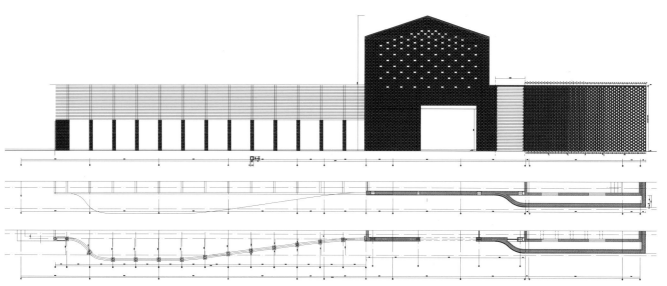

"We wanted to create this museum as a really diversified experience for people," says Pei Zhu, principal of Studio Pei-Zhu. "Tom and I wanted to tackle the future contemporary art museum."[35] By "Tom," Zhu means Thomas Krens, former director of New York's Solomon R. Guggenheim Foundation and a collaborator in both this museum and Studio Pei-Zhu's OCT Design Museum (see page 144).[36] By "the future contemporary art museum," Zhu might mean a really big museum with really big exhibition spaces.

Studio Pei-Zhu's 646,000-square-foot Minsheng Museum of Contemporary Art reuses a former Panasonic factory just north of Beijing's 798 Art Zone. While not as big as Beijing's National Museum of China (see page 30) and Shanghai's China Art Museum, the Minsheng's exhibition spaces rival those of almost any other museum. These include a second-floor gallery with almost 108,000 square feet and what Zhu calls a "no-height-limit exhibition space"—an unroofed area carved into the building and referencing a Chinese courtyard. A black-box space for performances with a forty-six-foot ceiling can open onto this courtyard through a door like that of an airport hangar.

The existing three-hundred-meter-long electronics plant gave the new museum its horizontal dimension. A vertical insertion is the museum's key addition. "In terms of the architecture, I wanted to keep the horizontal piece," says Zhu, "and then we crashed into the piece with a rock to stimulate this industrial building." A cluster of three rectangular forms made of dark gray recycled aluminum and cut with skylights slams into the low-lying concrete factory. The atrium that results from this impact is sliced with diagonal ramps and stairways used both for circulation and for amphitheater-like seating. Its cavernous volume turns the lobby into its own performance space.

From the outside, the vertical implant appears like a sculpture as much as a work of architecture, and like a geometrized meteor as much as a circulation space. This sculptural quality is not surprising from Zhu, who has described his design philosophy in this way: "First of all, I think architecture is a type of art; secondly, your personal bias is based on the future and the present; and finally, the source of your inspiration should come from nature."[37]

Zhu's artful museum is being developed by the China Minsheng Banking Corporation, the same art-loving entity behind three previous museums in China, including one in Shanghai, featured on page 112.[38] Programming for its Beijing museum has been ambitious. Its pre-opening plans have involved using fifty-four thousand square feet of gallery space to exhibit Chinese contemporary art, including works by Huang Yong Ping and Wang Guangyi. It also has planned to acquire and commission international works and stage exhibitions of foreign artists, including Anselm Keifer.[39] For Krens and Zhu, it seems "the future contemporary art museum" means a big space filled with equally big names.

MINSHENG MUSEUM OF CONTEMPORARY ART

STUDIO PEI-ZHU | BEIJING, 2013

TOP:
Exterior rendering showing vertical aluminum insertions into old factory

BOTTOM:
Interior rendering showing stairway that can be used as seating

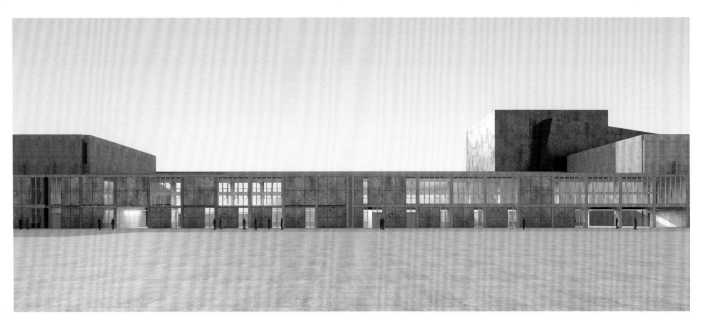

TOP:
Rendering of detail of facade

CENTER LEFT AND RIGHT:
Rendering of no-height-limit exhibition space

BOTTOM LEFT:
Rendering of skylit interior

BOTTOM RIGHT:
Former Panasonic factory before renovation

OPPOSITE

TOP:
First floor plan

CENTER:
South elevation

BOTTOM:
Sections

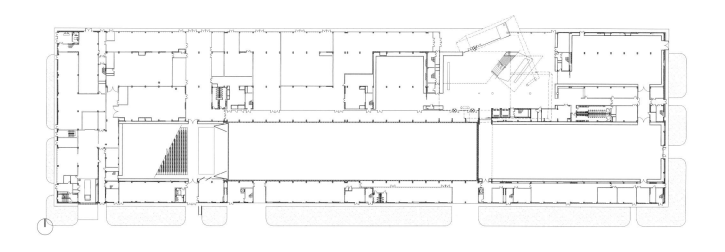

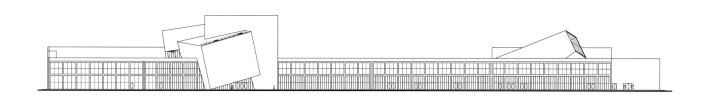

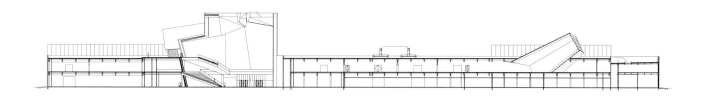

New Poly Plaza contains twenty-four stories of office space for the China Poly Group Corporation. This state-owned company specializes in "military and civilian trade and business, real estate development, culture and arts business, investment and exploitation in mineral resource field as well as civilian explosive materials and blasting service."[40] While Poly's "blasting service" may not have influenced Skidmore, Owings & Merrill (SOM) in the design of its corporate headquarters, its "culture and arts business" reads loud and clear. An eight-story, faceted form designed to accommodate galleries, performance spaces, a cinema, and an art auction room seems to pop out of the glass main facade. Brian Lee, design partner at SOM, describes the insertion as "a beautifully crafted curio box of Chinese art protected in a glazed lantern structure."[41] Wooden enclosures allow for light-controlled environments and set the form off from the light-filled atrium around it.

At the top of the lantern, Poly Art Museum holds court. A small collection showcases quality, not quantity. Two rooms contain exquisite examples of bronzes and Buddhist stone sculptures. A double-height space houses the museum's prize possessions: bronze animal heads from the zodiac fountain originally located in Beijing's Old Summer Palace. In 2000 Poly bought tiger, ox, and monkey heads for a total of $4 million at auctions held by Christie's and Sotheby's.[42] A fourth head, representing a pig, was later donated to the museum.[43] These particular depictions of the animals might be familiar to Western audiences from Ai Weiwei's 2010–14 traveling sculpture project *Circle of Animals/Zodiac Heads*.[44] The stories surrounding both the originals and the reinterpretations suggest the importance of these heads and of repatriation of Chinese art to China.

Poly Art Museum is not only the aesthetic and ideological focus of New Poly Plaza, but also a key component in its construction. To span the 295-by-197-foot glass atrium wall, SOM might have used space frames. But the firm wanted a less intrusive structure, so it considered a cable-net wall, a construction it had used in the Time Warner Center in New York. Lee explains the gridlike system: "Cables span from the edges of the frame, and the glass is attached to those cables." Running cables the full distance of the wall would have increased the force on them and caused them to noticeably bend. To prevent this, the designers added cables to the lantern containing the museum and used it as an anchor or, as Lee puts it, "the stays in a sail." By removing the support columns, the lantern's weight could counterbalance the forces placed on the surface of the atrium wall. In this way, what started as a formal idea—to make the museum's shape pop from the building like an object in a picture frame—became a structural solution.

Detail of lantern cable

OPPOSITE

TOP LEFT AND
RIGHT:
Rear facade of
New Poly Plaza

BOTTOM LEFT:
Two of the
bronze animal
heads on display

TOP:
Bird's-eye view of
main facade

BOTTOM RIGHT:
Buddhist stone
sculptures at the
museum

BOTTOM:
Detail of lantern
cable

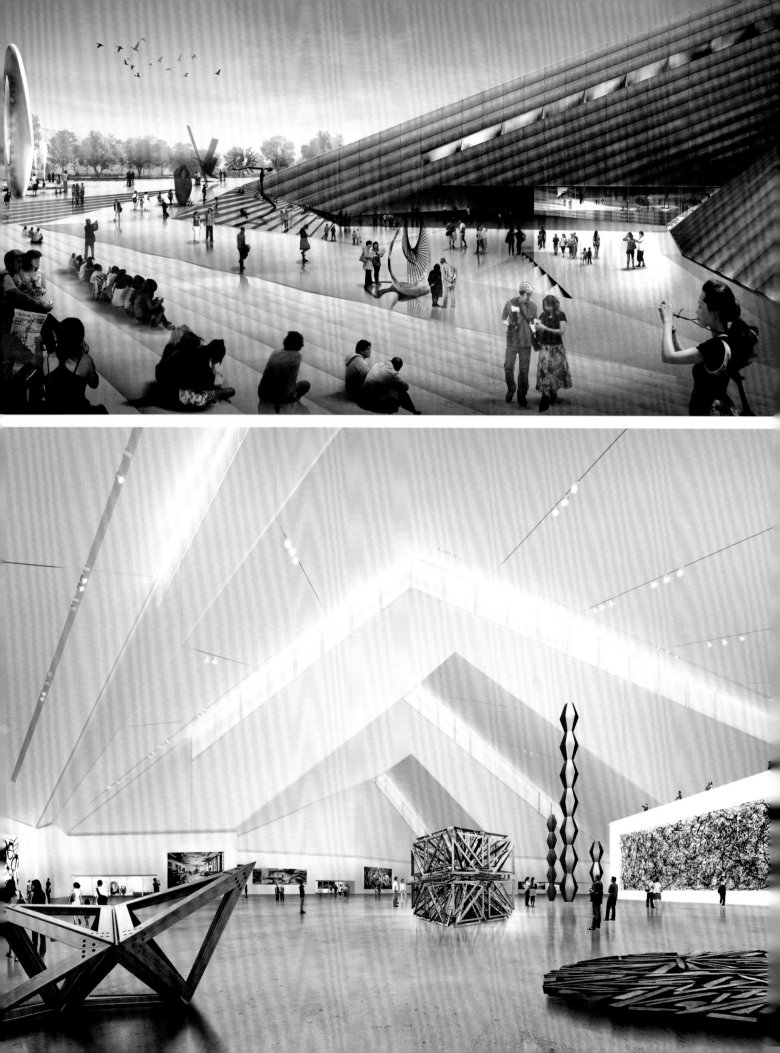

Datong Art Museum—with 344,000 square feet of space covered by a massive steel roof made of four linked pyramids emerging from a sunken plaza—creates an imposing scene. The composition, which Foster + Partners describes as "an erupted landscape," may remind visitors of the mountains that surround Datong.[45] This is a happy coincidence, according to Loretta Law, partner at Foster + Partners. The museum, she contends, was designed not as a reflection on topography but rather from the inside out. It found its form in its utility and its structure.[46]

"The reason it is a pyramidal form that spans across the site is because we were thinking about how we could get the most flexible gallery," says Law. Foster + Partners determined that the museum's central gallery should have the longest column-free span possible. In talking with their engineers, the architects decided to use a space truss with an inclined angle. And then they designed the roof with four folds instead of one, to extend the building to the site lines and to open it out to three neighboring buildings in Datong's new cultural center.[47] Law summarizes, "The idea of these ridges came about through initially wanting to create the most challenging, large-spanning structure to offer a very grand gallery."

This grand gallery, Law says, is necessary to accommodate future exhibitions. Like many new museums in China, the Datong Art Museum was designed without an existing collection as form giver: no *Mona Lisa*s requiring flat, white walls; no *David*s wanting tall, vaulted space. Without specific art to guide decision making, Foster + Partners assumed one thing: the art of the future would be big. "Artists have moved from historical painting and sculpture and now are much more involved in installation art, performance art, and digital art," says Law. "For all of these, the medium itself doesn't prescribe a limitation to the size of the art." Large gallery spaces allow for large art. They might even influence art. "The scale of the space could actually contribute to how artists respond to the space," says Law.

To allow for the public participation that has become a common element of contemporary art, the museum includes an exterior amphitheater, which Law refers to as an "urban living room." This sloping area in the site's northeast corner leads to the building's entrance. From the amphitheater, people can look into a children's gallery, one of the few areas of the museum with natural lighting. Two skylights bring additional light into public spaces. The architects chose to hide these skylights from outside view so as to maintain the impression of a solid roof.

That impregnable roof is faced in Chinese weathering steel. Foster + Partners had considered other materials, including ceramic and stone, but decided that weathering steel would be best both for its material properties and for its connotations. "Datong is a fairly harsh city because of the very cold, dry winter and hot summer," says Law. "The weathering steel gives a sense of harshness as a material, and it gives a more industrial feeling." Ceramic and stone, by comparison, seemed too fragile and too difficult to maintain. Law mentions the cleaning they would require. She does not mention that Datong, a coal-mining center, is considered one of China's most polluted cities.[48] In designing the Datong Art Museum—with its large, folded roof meant to corrode and weather attractively—Foster + Partners may not have been looking to the city's natural surroundings. But it seems the architects considered Datong's true nature—its industrial core.

TOP:
Rendering of view from the museum's "urban living room"

BOTTOM:
Rendering of interior of grand gallery

TOP:
Rendering of
bird's-eye view

—

BOTTOM AND
OPPOSITE
BOTTOM:
Construction of
structural frame,
December 2012

Unless you deal in coal, you probably have not heard of the capital of Shanxi Province. Taiyuan's new "Cultural Green Island" aims to change that. Its new collection of five cultural institutions—a theater, concert hall, library, and two museums—call for attention on a prominent site along the rerouted Fen River. Early massing guidelines for the five buildings render them as shapes from high-school geometry class—cube, pyramid, cylinder, and so on. For the archaeological museum, Paul Andreu, best known for his egg-shaped National Centre for the Performing Arts in Beijing, used inverted cones.[49] The shape suggested for the Taiyuan Museum of Art appears to be a tetradecahedron. But the actual museum designed by Preston Scott Cohen is much more complex than that. "You could say it's not being a good team player," jokes Cohen. "It decided to become part of the site rather than be one of the five buildings."[50]

This is not to say that Cohen is not fond of geometry. In fact, geometry is practically his calling card.[51] But his work is not as simple as inverted cones: Cohen is more interested in seventeenth-century projective geometry.[52] Twenty-first-century parametric software, in place of the compasses and protractors of his predecessors, allows him to build his studies into complex forms such as that in Taiyuan. "Basically, it's a series of hyperbolic parabolas stitched together as a composite to imply the overall form of a quatrefoil," he says. "And then the hyperbolic parabolas are broken down into even finer constituent elements: folded-plate geometry and panelization, where hyperbolic parabolas are composed of quadrangular flat panels." When this description elicits dead silence, he kindly adds, "It's a continuous process of transforming curvature into flatness" so that the quatrefoil can be surfaced with stone.

According to Cohen, the museum was designed from the inside out, with the intention of the interior and exterior becoming a single form. The 350,000-square-foot building was too large for a single focus. "It's so unwieldy and so vast," says Cohen. "So the question was, would there be a way to give definition to the outside and the inside so that one could somehow comprehend the whole building?"

The design attempts to do so by ringing a sequence of galleries around dual foci: a central outdoor courtyard and a large interior atrium. Visitors navigate a ramp that allows them to see glimpses of their path through the museum. These visual connections do not necessarily correspond to physical connections, as detours interrupt the flow. What Cohen calls "continuous and discontinuous promenades" might seem frustrating to some, but to him they compel museumgoers to "discover how to complete the journey." Breaks in the path allow alternative routes that might skip some galleries entirely. A path drives the exterior's composition as well, allowing people to pass through the building instead of into it in a "James Stirling in Stuttgart way," says Cohen.

The museum's low-lying form is designed to be a threshold between the Fen River and the land beyond. "Most of the buildings [in the Cultural Green Island] sit on their sites as big objects, with monumental stairs and mounded landscapes," says Cohen. "This building is more like an extension of the ground. The way it lies on the site, it looks like a slug or some kind of animal on the ground." A prominent element containing a restaurant cantilevers from the slug.

This cantilever and some large spans required that the building be made of steel. A steel structural frame supports a lighter steel frame, which in turn supports half-inch-thick Chinese granite panels. Cohen says these panels are often used in China for skyscraper facades. He used them here to give the facade the appearance of a single unified form rather than a smattering of pieces. The panels' large sizes (up to 21.5 square feet each) and their reflectivity might make them appear to be metal. But the stone is so flat that it does not have the bent effect of metal, says Cohen. This means that his complex geometry can carry over from design to building.

If it seems improbable that a quatrefoil building could be built on Taiyuan's Cultural Green Island, it is just as improbable that it was commissioned at all. In 2007, when a competition for the project was held, Cohen was not a known entity in China. He had just begun working on the Tel Aviv Museum of Art, but had no real record of built achievement. He had not even been invited to the competition, but rather had received it as a handoff from Steven Holl's too-busy office. Cohen had only three weeks to put together a proposal. "I still don't know how it was possible that I won," he says. "I think it really has to do with [Taiyuan's vice mayor] Geng Yanbo's vision of having something new and original." Geng is currently mayor of Datong, Shanxi's second-largest city, where Norman Foster is building a museum (see page 58) and Cohen a library that promise to put Datong, like Taiyuan, on the map.

TOP:
View of the Taiyuan Museum of Art from the Fen River

BOTTOM:
View showing restaurant cantilever

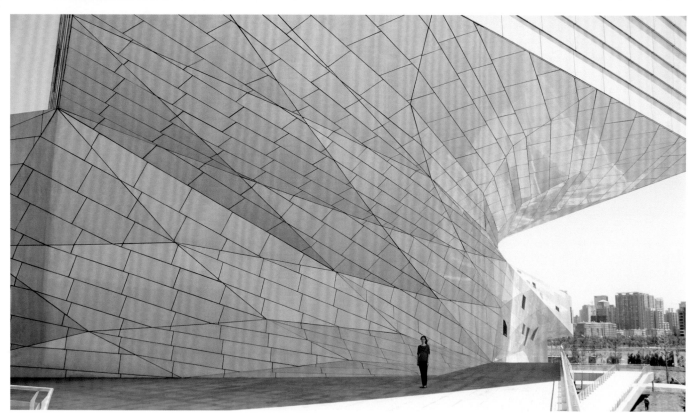

TOP:
View of the
folded-plate
geometry of the
granite facade

BOTTOM:
Exterior path
through the
museum

OPPOSITE

TOP:
First floor plan

BOTTOM:
Elevations

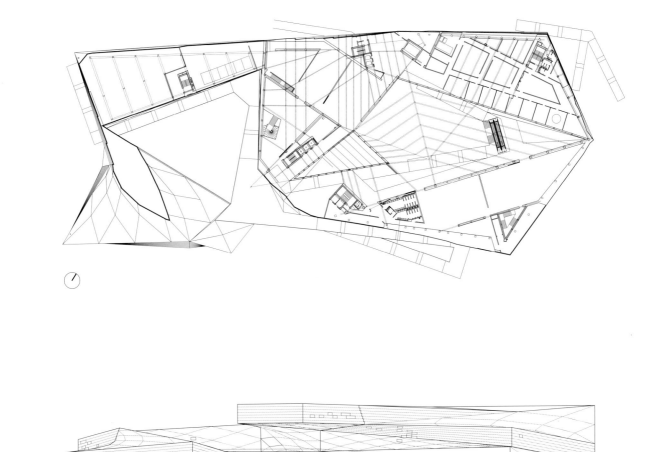

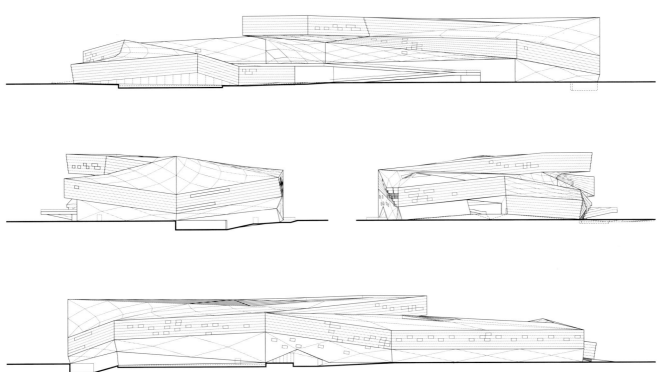

W hen we first arrived there, it was very raw land," says Xu Tiantian, principal of DnA Design and Architecture. "There were no people. There was a swan in the lake—very beautiful. We found a rabbit on the site."[53] Xu is talking about Kangbashi New Area, a new district of the Inner Mongolian city of Ordos, plunked down in the middle of the Gobi Desert. Kangbashi is not known for its rabbits. Rather, it is a much-publicized dream city for a population of five hundred thousand, fueled by Ordos's coal money.[54] That dream included the "Ordos 100," a 2007 plan for one hundred international architects to build one hundred villas, which so far has resulted in nothing more than a 2012 documentary and many pretty renderings.[55] Still, a large amount of architecture and infrastructure has been built (if not occupied) in Ordos.[56]

Xu was not surprised by the extent and pace of the building. In fact, her design for the Ordos Art Museum acknowledges that there will be growth around the site. "Even though it was very wild land at the time, we knew the whole development would change into a more urban situation," she says. While the museum is across a lake from the denser, more photographed center of Kangbashi, it already has a complex of artist studios by Ai Weiwei and other buildings as neighbors. The site's developer plans additional cultural facilities along with residential and commercial buildings.

The development sits on high ground— rough terrain compared with the flattened tabula rasa of the new town center below. The museum's form follows the site's wildness in a three-dimensional figure 8, which DnA's website associates with "a desert viper winding over the dunes."[57] Xu mentions a different origin. The shape, she says, follows the site's topography—going up and down and around as the ground does. DnA adds additional elevation to the building at the cross point of the 8, where one form bridges over another. The crossing not only accentuates the building's three-dimensionality but also frees up ground space below.

A view of the evolving cityscape of Kangbashi is part of the ride. Roughly one-third of the museum's exterior is glazed, and so on the way from entrance to exit visitors get a glimpse of construction sites and constructed sites as well as the art. "The museum isn't a self-enclosed art space," says Xu. "It's more like a journey on this site—a journey you take together with art." The journey does not form a complete figure 8, but rather is interrupted by an indoor-outdoor courtyard. DnA intended that museumgoers not end their tour where they began, but arrive at a public space open to even more views.

The museum's form is executed in a variety of materials. There is wood on the ceilings and floors of the courtyard, glass and blue slate on the exterior, and drywall and more blue slate on the interior. (Xu notes this stone is a common material in China: "It's on the floor of the Forbidden City.") The mix of ingredients creates unexpected angles and configurations. "With this museum," says Xu, "whatever you perceive is happening here will be part of the show."

The opening exhibition at the Ordos Art Museum—*Arrogance and Romance*, curated by Alexander Ochs and Tian Yuan—could be read as an expression of Ordos's ambitions.[58] It featured both Chinese artists and Andy Warhol, likely the first Warhol to be seen in Inner Mongolia. Xu admits that a show like this might seem surprising. "If you consider it in a smaller context, it seems weird," admits Xu. "But if you put it in a larger context—the ambition, what Ordos is going through—I think it's what they want. That's what their fantasy is about." She continues, "So it's not only about this individual Andy Warhol in the museum. It's also about the story of the museum and about Ordos as a city."

View showing
bridge above
indoor-outdoor
courtyard

OPPOSITE

TOP:
Exterior view

————

BOTTOM LEFT:
Interior view
showing mix of
materials

————

BOTTOM RIGHT:
Interior view of
skylit gallery

TOP:
Elevational
diagram

————

CENTER:
Second floor
plan

————

BOTTOM:
First floor plan

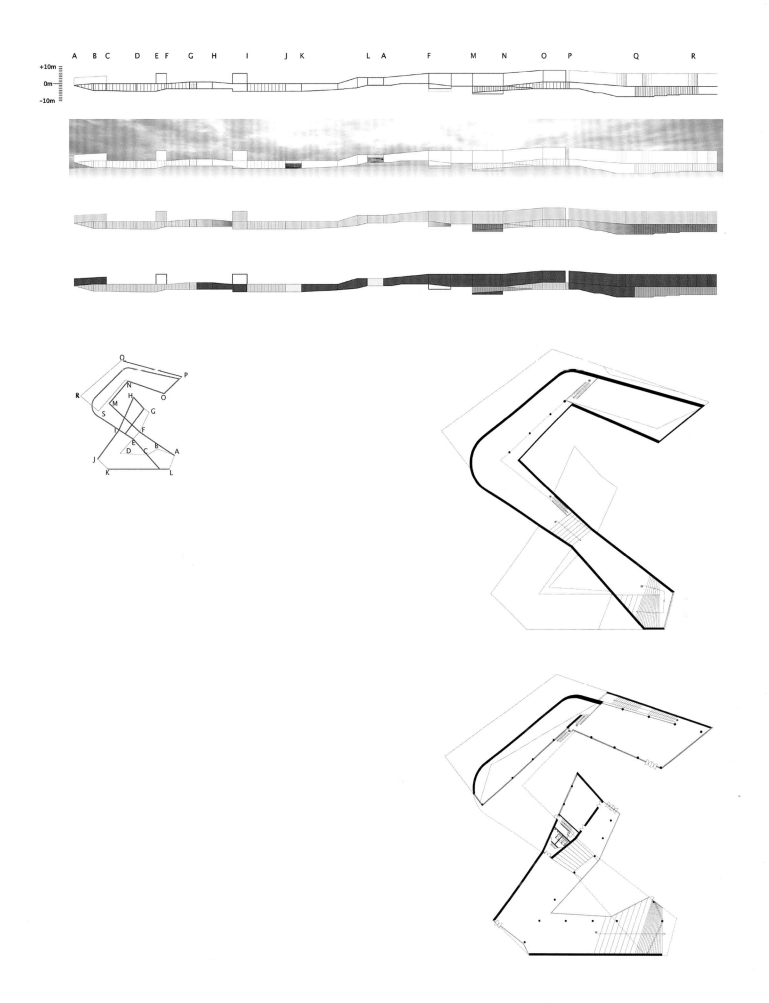

As the second major museum in a new city in the Gobi Desert, MAD Architects' Ordos Museum presents itself as a self-contained pod.[59] MAD's website identifies Buckminster Fuller's "Dome over Manhattan" as the inspiration for its defensive design.[60] But when pressed on this, Ma Yansong, principal of MAD, admits, "I don't know what the Manhattan dome intended to do, but I was inspired by a science-fiction movie about the end of the world. People can live only inside the dome; outside is a virus." He continues, "I was thinking, this city around our site won't stay a clean landscape. Some virus will grow, so we must protect what's inside."[61] Whatever the museum's inspiration, its intention is clear: to separate its cultural island from the burgeoning construction of Ordos's Kangbashi New Area.

Ordos Museum's aluminum-clad, virus-deflecting shell has been described as "a large undulating blob," "a natural, irregular nucleus," and a "building that seems like it has landed on the earth."[62] For Ma, the much-discussed form is secondary to the architectural idea. "I think the imagination comes first," he says. "You have to know what kind of atmosphere, what kind of space you want. And then you master the shape, material, technology, whatever. Everything combines to make this atmosphere."

Ma describes his intended atmosphere: "a new building responding to the history of the landscape." This means a landscape of sand dunes, which, Ma says, is central to the character of the Mongolian people. In fact, MAD created artificial hills on the museum site, because the wild landscape that existed when Ma first visited Kangbashi had been bulldozed to build a classically composed master plan. The museum, then, is "a very abstract object landing on this landscape," says Ma. "When you go there [the atmosphere] feels very, very strong. You walk on that slope, and there's a building coming right above you. Those horizontal lines on the facade feel like wind or the horizon of the landscape." By injecting an unfamiliar structure into a very old culture, Ma hoped to develop a new culture for a new place.

These ideas, coming out of MAD's Beijing-based firm, were not an easy sell in the Inner Mongolia Autonomous Region. Ma recalls the comments of some jurors for the 2005 design competition. "People said, 'You should do this because this looks like a traditional Mongolian tent [*ger*]' or 'that because it's similar to the Sydney Opera House.'" He continues, "I think their main challenge was how they could build a museum that would reference local culture." (One might note that "local" is relative; Han Chinese outnumber Mongolians by four to one in Inner Mongolia.)[63] "You always hear, 'This is local architecture. You should learn from their old technology. You should build small and learn to use the local material,'" Ma says. "But local culture is also developing. It has its own future. This kind of thing is a challenge for them. It's also a challenge for China."

Like many city museums in China, the Ordos Museum has a broad definition of "culture." Exhibits in its nine galleries range from fine art to dinosaur bones. Visitors enter up a long, wide stairway, through a low, curved doorway, into a cavernous space with galleries cut into glass-reinforced gypsum walls. Openings in the aluminum skin are reserved for public areas; it seems dinosaur bones do not benefit from natural lighting. The building also contains extensive offices for museum staff and Ordos's cultural department. A large south-facing window brightens the offices' wood-faced, multistory lobby.

Ordos Museum, says Ma, exhibits an "absence of today." The building might look futuristic to some people and like something from the past to others. Still, contemporary materials and structure—along with the latest 3-D modeling—allowed MAD's vision to be realized. These are not so important to Ma. The design, he claims, focuses on the space and the light. "Every building has a material; every building uses some technology. But they're not the key, the soul of architecture," he says. "Technology is outdated very quickly. But architecture should be more timeless."

View of museum on artificial hill

TOP:
View toward
entrance
——
BOTTOM LEFT:
Lobby in office
area
——
BOTTOM RIGHT:
View of interior of
exhibition area

OPPOSITE

TOP:
Second floor
plan
——
CENTER:
First floor plan
——
BOTTOM:
Section

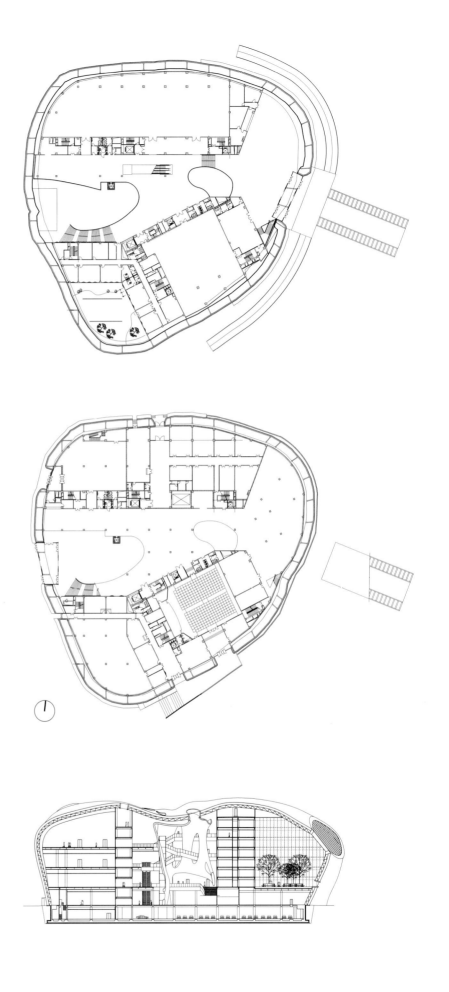

I t's like an urban plan," says Steven Holl. "The base is the city, and then out of the city rises some iconic figure."[1] He refers to the halves of his Sifang Art Museum as a diagram of dualities. The city and the figure. The ramble and the directed route. The heavy concrete and the light steel frame. (He could add the yin and the yang, but he does not.)

Still, Holl acknowledges some Sinology behind the design of the museum. "For me it is a meditation on the Western perspective in relation to space and China," he says. "So the building really is about space and about the movement through space and the perception of space." Holl's office publicizes its focus on space over other architectural considerations.[2] The firm's website describes its museums in the United States, Finland, Norway, Denmark, and France in spatial terms. In Nanjing that focus is especially clear, as the Sifang building is divided into two distinct spatial systems.

In the design of the building's base, Holl aimed for the effect of parallel perspective found in ancient Chinese paintings. He established this unique perspective, devoid of a vanishing point, in the museum's landscape, where walls set at irregular angles dissect a courtyard. "This ground tilts and these walls actually reverse the condition of the spatial perspective," says Holl. The heavy aesthetic of these walls continues into the museum's ground floor, which contains an entrance lobby, exhibition room, and auxiliary spaces.

Above this base rises a shape suggesting a paper lantern. Its Chinese form is not lost on Holl, but here he explores Western ideas of space. In the upper section, galleries spiral in a clockwise direction and end at a large window. "There's a kind of procession that loops around," he says, "and then you see the distant view, the perspective of the city of Nanjing."[3] Here the Western vanishing point, it seems, has become a viewing point.

Materials help to differentiate the two spatial systems. The concrete of the courtyard walls and the museum base was stained black for weather protection and for effect; Holl was attracted to the clear black-and-white delineation of Chinese ink washes. The formwork of the walls and base was lined with bamboo, which produced a rhythmic texture on the concrete. A bit of adaptive reuse was involved: the bamboo was harvested from the site, and the bricks that pave the courtyard came from old residences that were torn down elsewhere in Nanjing. In contrast to all this heaviness, a comparatively light steel frame and ultraviolet-resistant polycarbonate facade make up the spiraling figure.

The museum's open form suggests a gate, and this is not unintentional. It is the entrance building to the China International Practical Exhibition of Architecture (CIPEA), a permanent display of high-minded architecture across the river from downtown Nanjing. The CIPEA complex includes a conference center by Arata Isozaki, a clubhouse by Ettore Sottsass, and a hotel by Liu Jiakun.[4] In addition, twenty unique houses (ten by Chinese architects and ten by foreigners) were planned for the site. In the master plan, the museum opens onto the collection of houses by Wang Shu, David Adjaye, Kazuyo Sejima, and other noteworthy designers. This housing then opens onto a larger development of 125 luxury villas.[5]

The economics of building a museum in order to sell houses in order to sell villas seems to have gone awry.[6] At the time of this writing, nine years after CIPEA began, only a handful of houses have been completed, and villas are just beginning to take shape. The Sifang Art Museum, which was commissioned as an architecture museum, now plans to show paintings instead. It has not yet officially opened, but its bare walls can be seen by appointment. Holl seems unfazed by this. "For me, the building exists fine because it's about space and experience of space," he says. "It doesn't need to be filled with whatever in order to be a relevant thing."

There is another reason that this building works fine for Holl: it brought him to China. The museum, whose work was initiated in 2003, was the first of a string of Chinese projects for his office. "I build more in China than everything I did anywhere in the world, all added together, times a hundred or something," Holl says. While on site in Nanjing, he received a phone call about a commission in Beijing, for the Linked Hybrid apartment complex (2009). Holl has since completed buildings in Chengdu and Shenzhen, and many other projects are on the boards. "China's been good," he says. "So this little thing—it's a significant building on a lot of levels for me."

View of
courtyard and
floating galleries

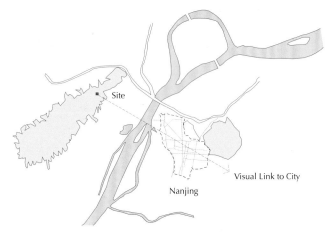

Site

Visual Link to City

Nanjing

CHINA 8 2603
S.N

TOP:
Second floor
gallery space

CENTER:
Rendering of view
of second floor
gallery

BOTTOM:
Rendering of view
of stairway from
first floor gallery

OPPOSITE

TOP:
Sections

BOTTOM:
Second floor
plan

78

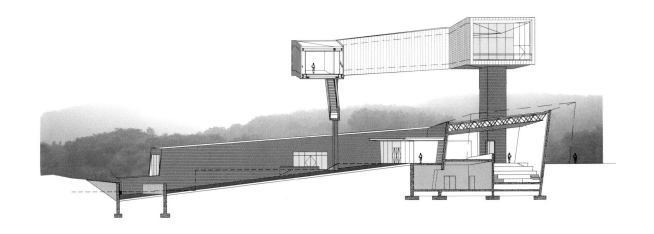

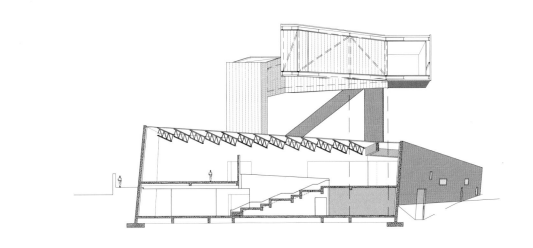

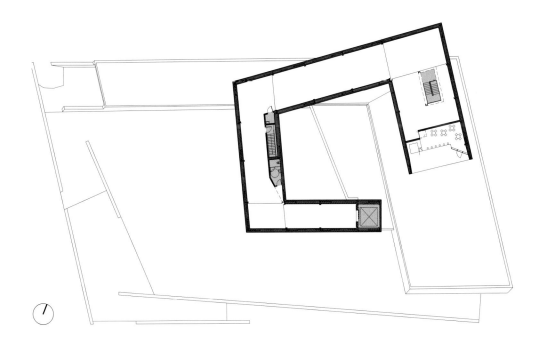

The buildings around Jiangsu Provincial Art Museum express Nanjing's diverse history. To the north is a palace used by a Ming Dynasty prince, a Qing Dynasty governor-general, and Sun Yat-sen, the "Father of Modern China."[7] At a corner of the former imperial gardens is "Nanjing 1912," a complex of Nationalist-era buildings redeveloped into bars and a Starbucks.[8] Across from this is a massive twenty-first-century library, whose riot of colors and shapes resembles an exploded material samples kit.[9]

In the middle of all this, the museum provides a bit of peace and quiet. "We wanted to keep it simple and very abstract," says Johannes Reinsch, partner at KSP Jürgen Engel Architekten. "We didn't want to make a lot of noise, because for the museum the most important things are the sculptures and paintings, not the architecture."[10] Reinsch describes the building itself as a piece of art, "a stone sculpture in the public space." The museum's two travertine boxes are elevated on a dark pedestal. Long, thin windows sliced into the stone create a rhythm seemingly unrelated to the floors behind them. "When you look at the building, you don't really know what scale it is," says Reinsch. "Maybe in other cities and in other environments, the building would have been less abstract."

KSP Jürgen Engel knew that a monolithic building would be a barrier to pedestrians in what had been an active public square and so laid a path through its center. Reinsch describes Nanjing's active, tree-lined streets: "This kind of atmosphere, we thought, somehow had to continue," he says. "This is the main reason we opened this building." Entrances on the site's northwest and southeast corners allow pedestrians to use the museum's lobby as a shortcut.

Reinsch characterizes the lobby as a canyon. Its strict vertical walls mimic the exterior facade. But a large skylight showers the multistory space with plenty of illumination. Reinsch says Nanjing's warm climate—unlike that of Beijing, where his firm built the National Library of China (2008)—allowed for the sunroom. "For us, Nanjing was always, compared to Beijing, a very green city with a lot of activity," he says. "In the northern part of the country the inside is more important, because the outside is not very friendly. You would never think to bring the outside to the inside there." Two U-shaped buildings, with exhibitions on the north side and administration on the south, surround the lobby. Fenestration follows function, with more windows for the office building than for the galleries.

KSP Jürgen Engel received this commission by winning an international competition. The firm has since won other museum competitions in China: the Tianjin Art Museum in 2009 and the Beijing Science Center in 2011. The 2006 competition for the Jiangsu Provincial Art Museum was its first victory. "Honestly, we were extremely surprised that we won," says Reinsch. He recalls numerous competition entries "with red cubes on top, floating over something. Somehow the governor said, 'This is what I want. It's simple. It's different.'"

View of skylit lobby

TOP:
View of northern
entrance

BOTTOM LEFT:
View from
northeast corner

BOTTOM RIGHT:
View of lobby
showing bridge at
upper floor

OPPOSITE

TOP:
Bird's-eye view

BOTTOM:
Site plan

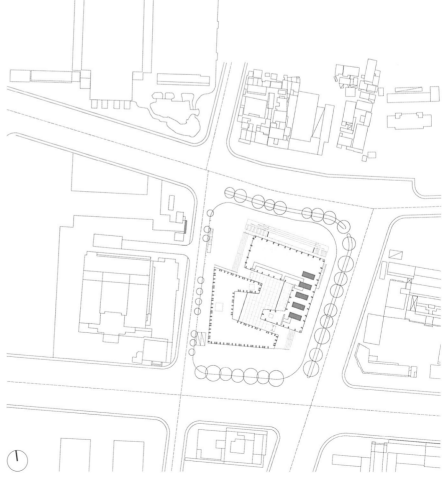

The decades-long career of I. M. Pei is punctuated with numerous museums. His East Building for the National Gallery of Art in Washington, DC (1978), pyramid at the Louvre in Paris (1989), and Rock and Roll Hall of Fame and Museum in Cleveland (1995) speak a similar cross-generational language.[11] Each high-modern specimen includes geometries as strict as the circular frames of Pei's signature eyeglasses.

For his first museum in China, completed when the architect was eighty-nine, Pei brought something new to his architectural language. "This was in Suzhou," says Chien Chung Pei, principal of Pei Partnership Architects and I. M. Pei's son. "The site was adjacent to one of the most important gardens in the historical area. There really wasn't, I don't think, any question in my father's mind but that he had to do something that was a continuation of the Suzhou tradition. And as his own style had evolved, he was able to bring that to bear in this project."[12]

The senior Pei had roots in Suzhou. His ancestral home, Lion Grove Garden, is two blocks south of the museum site, and he had visited the area on trips from his native Guangzhou. "It did have an influence on my work," he says.[13] This does not mean he replicated the buildings of his youth in the museum's design. "He didn't want to use anything traditional," says C. C. Pei, "but he wanted it to evoke the spirit of the tradition."

The Suzhou Museum looks like a montage of I. M. Pei's two traditions, with modernist forms wrapped in Chinese aesthetics, and vice versa. A dark roof, somewhat at odds with Pei's monochromatic modernism, is cast in granite instead of local tile. Wooden trim hides steel supports, favoring form over truth in materials. An indoor water feature, a potentially natural element, is formed from thin channels cut into a two-dimensional wall. Hexagonal windows frame views to the outside, a device borrowed from Chinese gardens, while diamond-shaped windows frame nothing but sky.

The museum includes Prince Zhong's Residence, a nineteenth-century complex that formerly housed the museum collection, and the re-creation of a pavilion from the Song Dynasty, hidden in the site's northeast corner. The latter was designed and built in collaboration with local people still practicing ancient building techniques. "It was my father's way of trying to allow people to understand what the purely traditional construction was like," says C. C. Pei.

At the heart of the modernist-traditionalist museum is its garden, designed as "a contemporary extension [of] and commentary" on the renowned sixteenth-century Garden of the Humble Administrator north of the museum site.[14] The gardens are connected only virtually, as walls prohibit a direct link. The key elements of the old garden—water, bridge, pavilion—take on a strict geometric form in the new one.

A less rigid object, an I. M. Pei sculpture dubbed *Range of Stones*, hugs the courtyard's north wall. C. C. Pei recounts the Suzhou tradition of scholar rocks that influenced the work. Locals would place a piece of limestone into Lake Tai, allow the water to carve away at it, and then, generations later, harvest it as a piece of sculpture. At the new museum I. M. Pei wanted not a single piece but an entire landscape of stone. "This is exactly what the Suzhou gardens were doing," says C. C. Pei. "The rocks were supposed to look like they were natural. But they were all completely built up and glued together." For the new collage, I. M. Pei and his craftsmen selected boulders, "sliced them up like bread," and then finished them with a blowtorch to achieve the final form.

Framed by a large picture window across from the entrance door, *Range of Stones* is the first thing visitors see. "In a Chinese garden, all the views are carefully constructed," says C. C. Pei. East of this entrance are the museum's offices, tearoom, and contemporary exhibition space. West is its collection of historical artifacts. The museum worked with James C. Y. Watt of the New York Metropolitan Museum of Art to curate the existing collection and integrate acquisitions. Still, C. C. Pei admits, "I don't think, to be honest with you, that people are going to go to Suzhou Museum just for the art." It is more likely that people will visit to see one of the final buildings designed by the Pritzker Prize–winning I. M. Pei. There they will encounter a work that is a complex vision of its singular author.

View from
garden

TOP:
Range of Stones in garden

OPPOSITE

BOTTOM LEFT:
Garden pavilion

TOP:
Night view from street

BOTTOM RIGHT:
View from neighborhood

BOTTOM:
Night view from garden

OPPOSITE

TOP:
Site plan with
Suzhou Museum
in dark gray
and the Garden
of the Humble
Administrator
above it

BOTTOM:
Section

TOP:
Interior of great
hall at entrance

BOTTOM:
Contemporary art
gallery

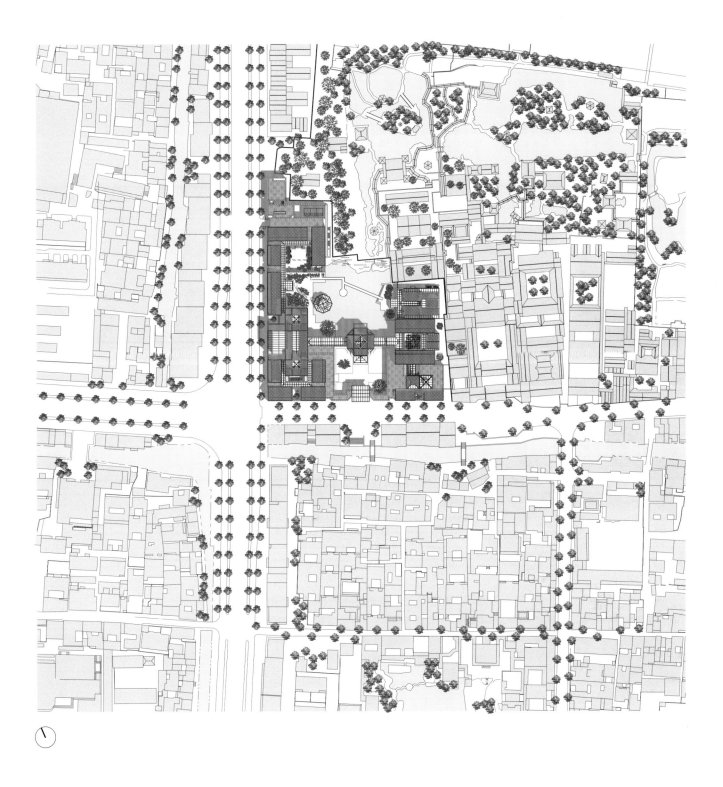

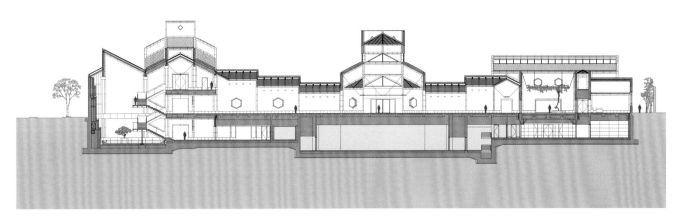

Just west of the Bund, Shanghai's riverfront curve of beloved historic buildings, the Rockefeller Group is refurbishing and redeveloping a six-block area.[15] David Chipperfield Architects is responsible for eleven of the buildings in the project's first phase, and its Rockbund Art Museum (RAM) was one of the first restorations completed. The building where RAM makes its home was formerly the Royal Asiatic Society (RAS) Building, an art deco beauty that was designed by Palmer & Turner in 1932 and served as a museum, library, and lecture hall for the British organization until 1952.[16]

The architects of RAM welcomed the opportunity that the RAS Building presented. "When we arrived, we were fascinated by the actual material, by the dignity of how buildings age," says Mark Randel, partner of David Chipperfield Architects, Berlin. "We wanted to keep that, and we wanted people to be able to see that this is an old building, not just a replica of an old building. I think that was something quite new when we started the project."[17]

Randel says his office was recommended to the Rockbund project by architect Ben Wood. Wood's Xintiandi, a 2001 shopping district that combines selective restoration with re-creation, is the more common model for reusing buildings in Shanghai.[18] In fact, other buildings in the Rockbund project follow Xintiandi's strategy.

"There is a tendency to keep old buildings in China," says Randel. "However, I think there is not so much a culture of keeping the actual material. Maybe it is true not only in China but in Asia that 'keeping' doesn't mean keeping the wood or keeping the brick. It could also mean—as in Japanese temples—rebuilding every so often. In China people are quite relaxed with that attitude. I'm not judging that, but it's a different culture."

Chipperfield's office took a more Western approach to restoring the RAS Building. It preserved not only its essence but also its details. Randel points to the front facade and its original bricks. "There's a tradition in Shanghai that they put a lot of paint on top," he says. "Then the brick cannot breathe and you get a lot of damage. We did only a very good cleaning job and repointing. But you can see the age of the facade."

The architects treated the rear facade differently. They wanted to keep the historic structure but needed to add a freight elevator and technical spaces, and so they extended the east elevation. "That extension was also an opportunity to give the museum a new face," says Randel. "Originally the building was looking only in one direction. But because of the new master plan, the inner space of this block becomes a public space. So by making this little extension you also get a back facade." The extension also gave the building a top-floor outdoor terrace, from which visitors today can watch the construction of the rest of the Rockbund project.

Because the RAS Building had already been used as a museum, the architects did little to its interior to make RAM. "We already had exhibition rooms," says Randel, "so we just had to adapt the existing structure to make it work as a modern museum." The architects reinforced the structure with carbon fiber, added a corner elevator, took out a skylight between the top two floors, and thickened exterior walls to create spaces for air conditioning. Otherwise, they kept as much of the original space as possible and restored rather than replaced many existing details, including windows, staircases, handrails, and terrazzo flooring.

In contrast to its historical home, RAM "dedicates its efforts to the study, exchange, and promotion of contemporary visual arts."[19] Liu Yingjiu, deputy director of RAM, describes how the museum's inaugural exhibition—Cai Guo-Qiang's *Peasant Da Vincis*—addressed the space. "Cai hung airplanes and submarines in the atrium, he planted grass on the fourth floor, and he put in live birds," says Liu. "He created a very sensual, fairy-tale atmosphere, in opposition to the very clean lines of the art deco style in the museum."[20] Liu recalls discussions between RAM and Chipperfield about that style. "The museum's view was mostly pragmatic," he says. "We were concerned about how to bring the artworks in. It was David who was more concerned about aesthetics."

West entrance

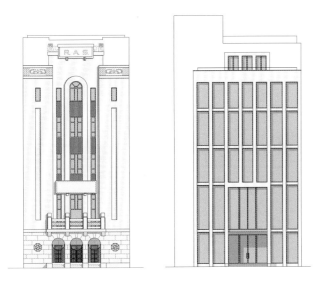

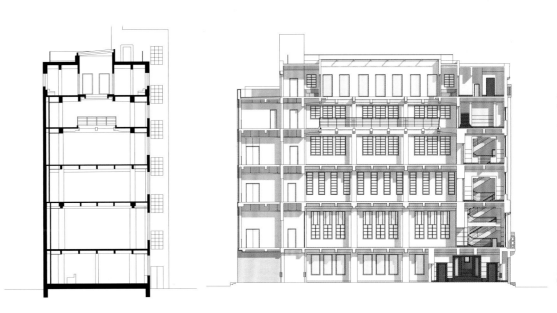

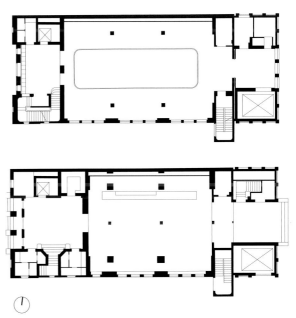

Shanghai is not known for preservation. While many of its art deco–era gems remain, many more of its historically significant buildings have been demolished to make way for skyscrapers. And so it is surprising that Atelier Liu Yuyang's design for the Shanghai Museum of Contemporary Art was a renovation project. It is more surprising still that the original building, a greenhouse designed by the Jiao Tong University Design Institute, was only a few years old. According to Liu Yuyang, principal of the eponymous studio, high heating and cooling costs and low ticket revenue made the greenhouse unsustainable. The local government that owned the property put it up for bid with the condition that the building not be destroyed. "That's the irony," says Liu. "If it were old, it might have been demolished. But as it was new, they didn't want to be perceived as wasteful."[21]

Shanghai MoCA sits in People's Square, home to several of the city's most important cultural institutions. When Liu received the commission, the park already contained three government-run museums: the Shanghai Art Museum (a 1934 structure that had served as a clubhouse for a racetrack), the Shanghai Museum (a 1996 behemoth whose design symbolizes "the ancient Chinese philosophy that the square earth is under the round sky"), and the Shanghai Urban Planning Exhibition Center (a 2000 building whose four flying roofs reference a magnolia).[22] While these museums may fall short in architectural brilliance, they make up for it with impressive collections. Shanghai MoCA would be a much different project—the first privately funded museum in Shanghai and a museum without a permanent collection. "We decided it would be different from a governmental museum," says Liu. "It would be much more open and transparent and fun."

The key component of this fun is the museum's sweeping interior ramp. Liu drew inspiration from both Frank Lloyd Wright's Guggenheim Museum and the on-ramps to Shanghai's intracity highways. MoCA's ramp helped solve a circulation problem left over from the original building. It also made a grand stage. In the evenings, when the museum hosts special events, it is lit by internal fluorescent tubes and becomes a place to see and be seen.

Building the seemingly simple ramp required specialized expertise. Liu called on his friend, the engineer Ronan Collins, to help design a system for the curved form to be supported on the building's existing columns and walls. Liu and Collins allowed the columns to interrupt the ramp at irregular intervals, so that visitors might feel as if they are walking amid trees. After two teams of contractors failed to build the design, Liu hired former workers from Shanghai's shipyards, who had no problem executing the complex curves.

Additional interventions at MoCA included creating a new entrance plaza, recladding concrete facades with Mongolian black stone, and using triangular glass to detail a new entrance and an enlarged third-floor restaurant. In all these gestures, Liu respected the greenhouse's original design. If the building had been older, he says, he would have designed a renovation that dramatically demonstrated what was new. But on this almost contemporary building, Liu used a subtly different language to identify his additions.

SHANGHAI MUSEUM OF CONTEMPORARY ART

ATELIER LIU YUYANG | SHANGHAI, 2005

View from northwest

OPPOSITE

TOP LEFT:
View of front
plaza

TOP:
Ramp from first
floor gallery

TOP RIGHT:
Detail of
landscaping

BOTTOM LEFT:
Second floor
children's area

BOTTOM LEFT:
First floor plan

BOTTOM RIGHT:
Interior detail

BOTTOM RIGHT:
South elevation
and section

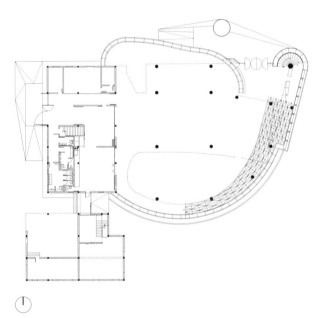

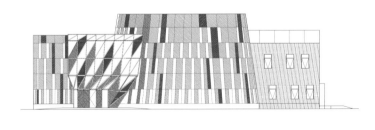

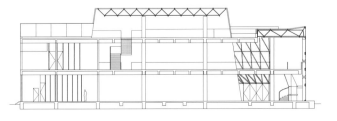

Visitors typically come to Zhujiajiao because of its history. A water town billed to tourists as "Shanghai's Venice," the area is picture-postcard pretty, with ancient canals and arched bridges and the souvenir stalls that these elicit.[23] A painting of the town at the entrance of the Zhujiajiao Museum of Humanities and Arts shows a field of pitched black tile roofs on cute white buildings.[24] A "you are here" spot marks the sole exception: the museum's boxy, contemporary structure.

When asked if building a novel design in a historic neighborhood created any problems, Zhu Xiaofeng, design principal of Scenic Architecture Office, says, "Of course there were."[25] In town meetings, residents complained about the museum's amount of glass, among other things. But Zhu and his client defended their essential design. To Zhu, the museum expresses the fabric of the old town in nonformal ways—in its courtyards, its color scheme, and its respect for what remains of its site's history.

The 19,375-square-foot museum is organized around a wooden staircase. Zhu compares its sculptural form to the center of a landscape or a "scenery catcher." (The literal translation of the Chinese name of Zhu's firm is "mountain water show," which suggests its priorities.) The second floor has five gallery spaces and five outdoor courtyards. "These courtyards give the building space to breathe and help people inside to communicate with nature and with the old-town scenery," says Zhu. "I hope the overall impression in your mind after you visit the museum is that you can't tell it's one modest space. It should be a continuous montage of all the interior space and exterior space."

The museum's white exterior walls match the color of neighboring buildings. Its flat roofs, made of French zinc instead of Chinese tile, help maintain the local palette. "It's a modern building, but it's gray, it's white, it's black, and it's a pure glass color," says Zhu. The color, he says, "never challenges the town."

The site where the museum now stands once housed a temple that was demolished in the 1950s. What remains is an almost-five-hundred-year-old ginkgo tree, "the second-oldest tree in Shanghai," according to Zhu. Actually, there are two ancient ginkgos, but one has been fading since the construction of a bank across the street. Townspeople believe the bank's basement had cut off nutrients to the tree's roots. Scenic Architecture Office omitted the basement from its design to alleviate the town's concerns about additional damage.

The large glass window of a room designed as a cafe and library overlooks the ginkgos. Its pitched roof is angled to match the pitch of the trees. Zhu calls this space a "memory room." When the temple was on the site, he says, one can imagine that people had direct contact with the ginkgos. With the new museum, "We provide a new way to enjoy them, which is to keep a distance from them," says Zhu. "Because in China there is no religion anymore [*laughs*], maybe nature, pure nature, can be something that can save our heart."

Evening views toward the entrance

TOP:
First floor atrium
with "scenery
catcher" stairway
———
BOTTOM LEFT:
Gallery space
———
BOTTOM RIGHT:
View from cafe
and library to
ginkgo tree

OPPOSITE
———
TOP:
East courtyard on
second floor
———
CENTER:
Water courtyard
on second floor
———
BOTTOM:
Site axonometric

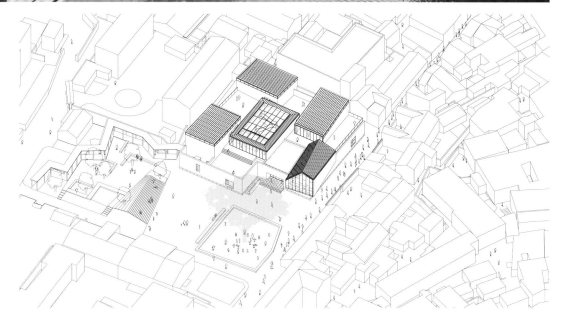

Himalayas Art Museum is part of the multifunction Himalayas Center in Shanghai's Pudong New Area. Arata Isozaki & Associates designed a hotel on the north end of the long center, an office building on the south, and an entrance space between them. The museum sits a bit off-center, with its lobby in the entrance area and its galleries in the office zone. "Isozaki-san accepted this project because of the museum," says Hu Qian, partner of Isozaki + HuQian Partners. "The client said he wanted to build the museum in the center and put all the supporting commercial space around it."[26]

Isozaki's 2007 sketch for the center shows the three distinct heights of the offices, hotel, and entrance: mama bear, papa bear, baby bear. The site plan shows their distinct spatial organization: square within square, circle within square, amorphous something. But the project is more obviously cut into two rather than three. "First, Isozaki-san set a hundred-foot platform," says Hu. "Above the platform is designed for the urban scale—for a bird's-eye view or for when you're driving past. Under the platform is for the human scale."

The space above is very businesslike. Hu describes each tower as "a shining cube floating in the air." The north and south ends below the platform are inscribed with something that seems familiar. "They are not Chinese characters, but they look like them," says Hu. In the center is an organic composition, standing in defiant opposition to its regular neighbors. Its treelike columns cannot help but suggest the work of Antoni Gaudí. And like Gaudí's columns, Isozaki's are based on physical forces rather than aesthetics alone. Gaudí hung weights from chains to develop his curves.[27] Isozaki used computer modeling with the help of the structural engineer Mutsuro Sasaki. Sasaki's Extended Evolutionary Structural Optimization allowed the architect to position the columns, the engineer to model the forces on them, and each of them to repeat until they created a design that was both aesthetically pleasing and structurally smart.[28]

Despite the seeming incongruity of this organic insertion—or maybe because of it—the Himalayas Center is a unified design. According to Hu, Isozaki had hoped that the management of the hotel, offices, and museum would be similarly unified. That did not happen. What was planned as office space has been realized as a mall. A Shanghai magazine labels the museum a "modern art gallery based in a Pudong shopping mall."[29] This is not the elevated position Isozaki had in mind. The hotel opened in 2011 and the mall in 2012. As this book goes to press, the museum and an adjoining theater are scheduled to officially open in 2013.[30] "Maybe they will change the museum to the gallery market—we don't know," says Hu. "I don't think the museum will become Isozaki's hope for a museum." Art lovers will be sad for the lost opportunity. But architecture fans will be happy that the mere idea of a museum brought Isozaki's work to Shanghai

View toward museum entrance

TOP LEFT:
Detail of facade, showing a pattern reminiscent of Chinese characters

TOP RIGHT:
Detail of entrance facade, showing the vertical division at one hundred feet

BOTTOM LEFT:
Museum gallery, installation view of *Tony Cragg: Sculptures & Drawings*

BOTTOM RIGHT:
Treelike columns at the building's central entrance

OPPOSITE

TOP:
Roof plan

CENTER:
East elevation

BOTTOM:
Sketch of east elevation

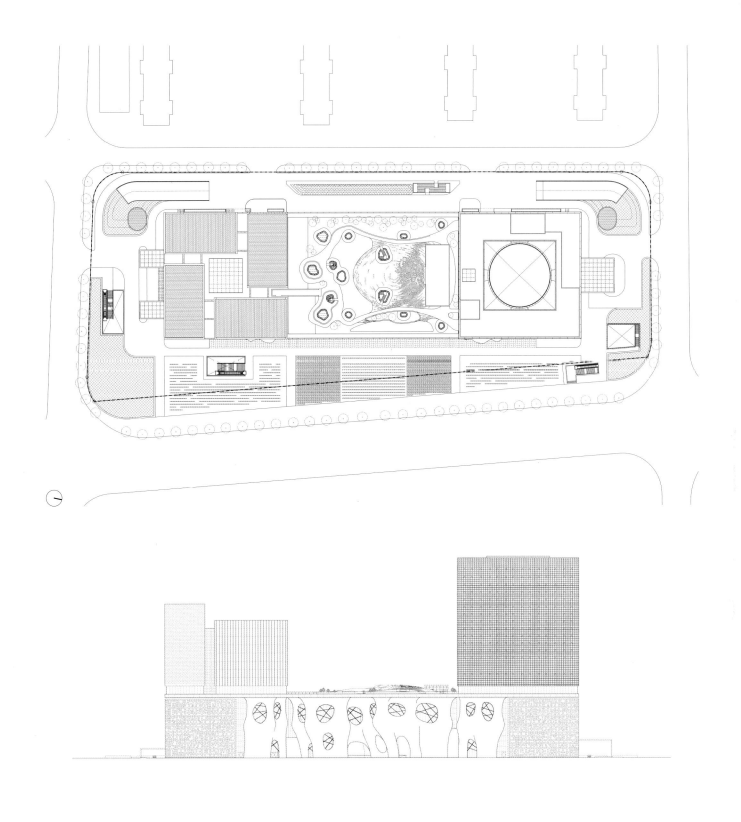

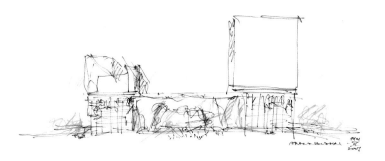

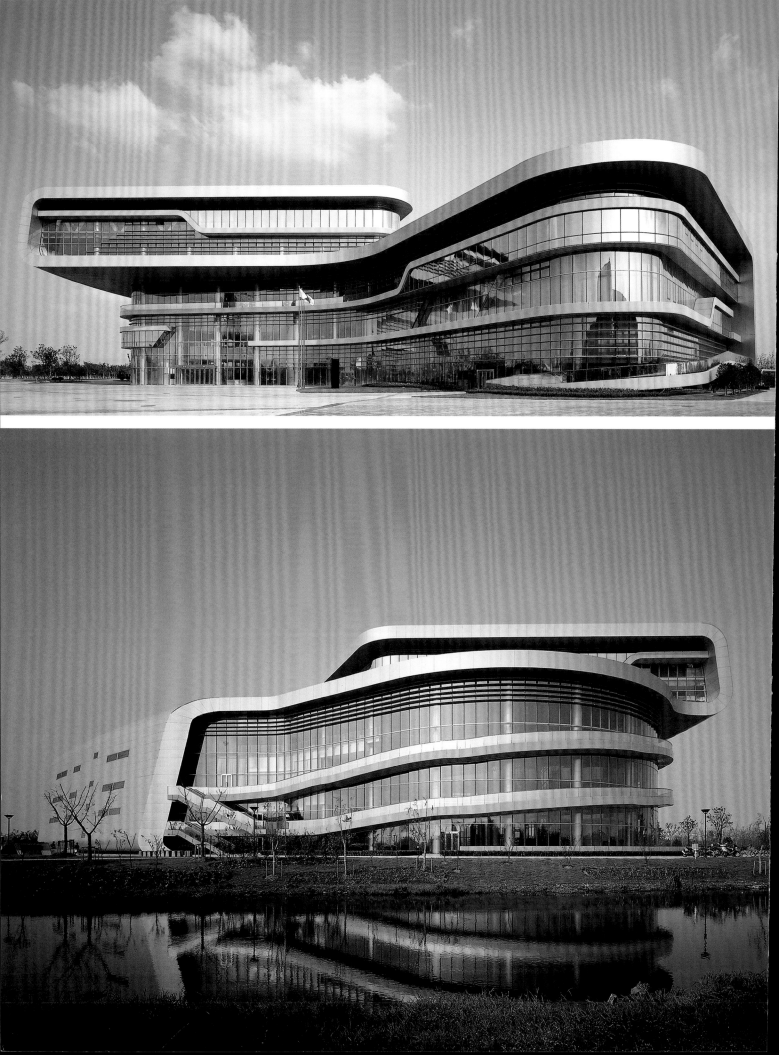

Shanghai Auto Museum is part of the greater Shanghai International Automobile City. This city and the adjacent Anting New Town were planned by the German firm Albert Speer & Partner (AS&P) for Shanghai's western Jiading District.[31] And Anting in turn is part of the 2001 "One City, Nine Towns" plan to redevelop outlying areas of Shanghai based on foreign models.[32] The other eight new towns include the Spanish-themed Fengcheng, Dutch-themed Gaoqiao, and English-themed Songjiang, which contains the "Tudor homes, Georgian townhouses, and Victorian warehouses" of Thames Town.[33] According to Harry den Hartog, editor of *Shanghai New Towns*, "A German theme was almost inevitable [for Anting], given the dominant position held by Volkswagen," which opened a plant in the area in 1984.[34]

Along with AS&P, the German firms Architekten von Gerkan, Marg und Partner; Auer+Weber+Assoziierte; and Braun & Schlockermann und Partner have built in the area.[35] Add to this list IFB Dr. Braschel AG, who designed both the Shanghai Auto Museum and the Shanghai Automobile Exhibition Center that faces it across a plaza. Considering the globalization of twenty-first-century architecture, it is difficult to label a design "German." But there is something about the museum's clean curved lines, shiny glass and aluminum facade, and bright orange color that seems Teutonic. Annette Lippmann, who was project architect for IFB Dr. Braschel AG and now runs her own firm, describes the design in this way: "The rounded shapes of the structures reflect the dynamic forms of a landscape and the themes of movement and speed. At the same time, the design symbolizes the image or detail of a car body that is partially skinned, carved, or opened. Thus the visitor is able to glimpse into this technological structure when approaching the museum."[36]

The dynamism of the design extends into the interior, where the entrance opens onto a sweeping ramp surrounding a large atrium. The ramp holds a collection of cars and can be used to move from one floor to another. Lippmann describes the circulation in automotive language: "Someone can use the elevators to come directly ('race') to a destination or may stroll ('cruise') along the ramps through the exhibition." The museum's main exhibition spaces currently house a "history pavilion" on the first floor and an "antique-car pavilion," filled with treasures from the California-based Blackhawk Collection, on the second floor. There are plans to expand exhibitions to the upper floors.

Atelier Brückner from Stuttgart designed the museum exhibitions for the exquisite collection, which includes auto prototypes from the early twentieth century, streamlined hood ornaments from the 1930s, Hongqi (red flag) sedans from the 1950s, American muscle cars from the 1970s, and twenty-first-century electric cars. The exhibition design imitates the dramatic movement-inspired lines of the architectural design. For both Brückner and Braschel, this was a first project in China. Uwe R. Brückner, creative director of his eponymous firm, says that the mix of German and Chinese participants fostered a good collaboration where "everybody learned from everybody."[37] He says, "The subject made it possible. Cars or mobility are more connecting content than other content." One might include residential content in that other content. The German-designed housing of Anting—like that of other Shanghai new towns—has not been so successful. The community projects to have twenty-eight thousand residents by 2020, but had only a few hundred in 2010.[38] German design, it seems, may be easier to accept in a single building than in an entire town.

SHANGHAI AUTO MUSEUM

IFB DR. BRASCHEL AG | SHANGHAI, 2006

TOP:
View toward west entrance

———

BOTTOM:
View toward rear

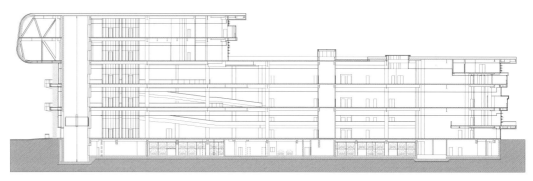

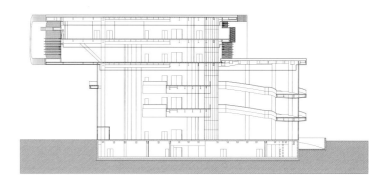

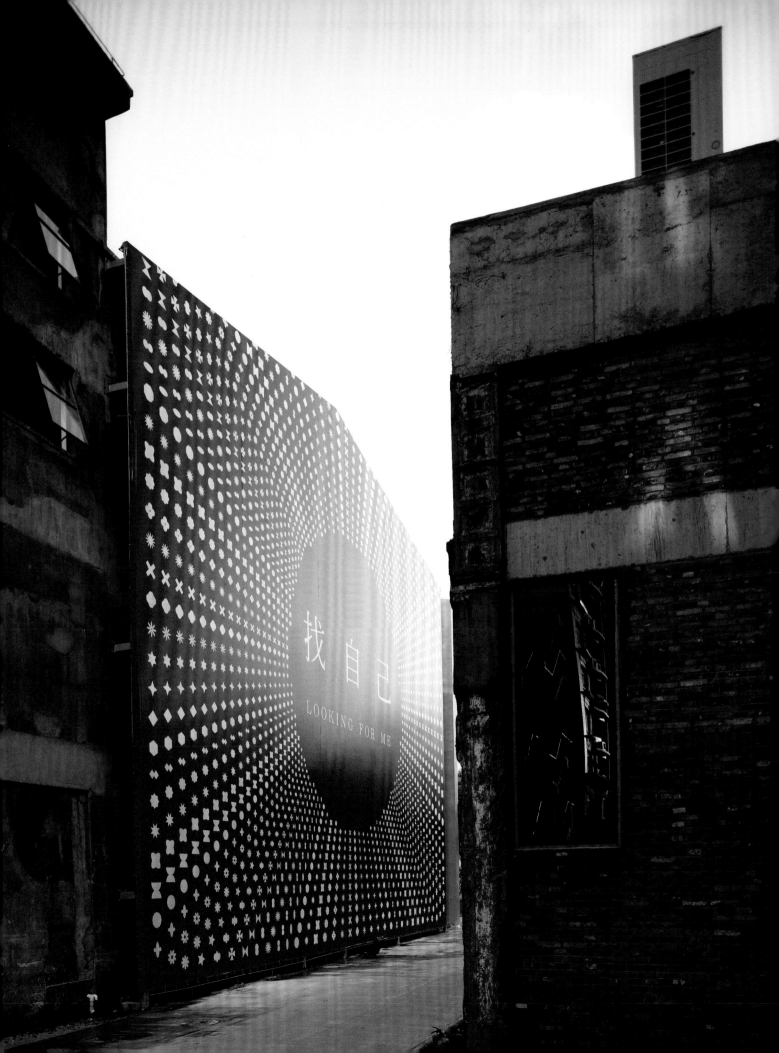

找 自己

LOOKING FOR ME

The buildings that once made up the Shanghai No. 10 Steel Factory now have a much more contemporary use: they have been converted into the creative industry park known as Red Town. Parks like these redevelop abandoned industrial buildings into art galleries, design shops, and offices for artistic entrepreneurs—architects, clothing designers, manga makers, and the like. According to the Shanghai government, "By the end of 2008, the city had seventy-five creative industry parks."[39]

Approach Architecture Studio was commissioned to transform Red Town's second-largest factory building into the Minsheng Art Museum. The factory's walls had been eroded by the acid used to process steel during the building's previous incarnation. Liang Jingyu, principal of Approach Architecture, was fond of the effect and proposed preserving it in the new museum. "I don't think anything we could add on would be better than the original facade," he says.[40] His client, China Minsheng Banking Corporation, was not receptive to the idea. "They're bankers, right? They also like buildings to wear suits," jokes Liang. "From my understanding, suits are equal to aluminum panels or some other kind of clean facade."

Why would a client acquire an old building only to hide its age under new facing? Liang, whose practice includes many renovations, recounts the fable "*Ye Gong Hao Leng*" (Lord Ye loves dragons). Ye professes his love of dragons. A dragon hears of this love, and comes to visit Ye, who runs away in fear. Ye is in love with the dragon's image, not the actual dragon. "Our clients might have this similar thing," says Jiang. "They might think it's cool to rent an industrial building. But they still prefer a more elegant style rather than a rough industrial feeling."

Approach Architecture's design for the Minsheng Art Museum aimed to balance "what they like and what we want to preserve," says Liang. For the facade, the architects designed an aluminum grill that both covers up and exposes the original wall. They supported their proposal with the fact that the new layer was sufficiently detached from the old building to create a usable space between the two. As the client would pay rent on only the interior square footage, the new facade grill offered free bonus space.

Liang says that for his renovation projects, the design of the facade is ultimately not so important, as long as it does not interfere with the new use. The interior design was more essential when converting a steel factory to an art museum. To create the interior space, Approach Architecture gutted two abutting extant buildings. It used one as a double-height gallery space and split the other into two floors of smaller galleries with a central island. Stairways and mechanical spaces hug the old walls. The architects left the interior surface of the walls raw. After the client took possession of the building, these were painted over. Liang admits, "My ultimate goal is not to achieve 100 percent of my design. I think this is unrealistic." Still, he says, "Maybe through my design I can help clients to understand or discover the beauty of an existing project."

MINSHENG ART MUSEUM
APPROACH ARCHITECTURE STUDIO | SHANGHAI, 2008

View from southeast

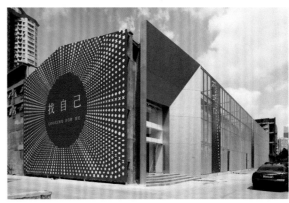

TOP:
Second floor
gallery

CENTER:
Former steel
factory prior to
renovation and
after the addition
of an aluminum
facade

BOTTOM:
First floor gallery
with original wall
finish

OPPOSITE

TOP LEFT:
View from
entrance lobby

TOP RIGHT:
View toward
main entrance

BOTTOM:
First floor plan

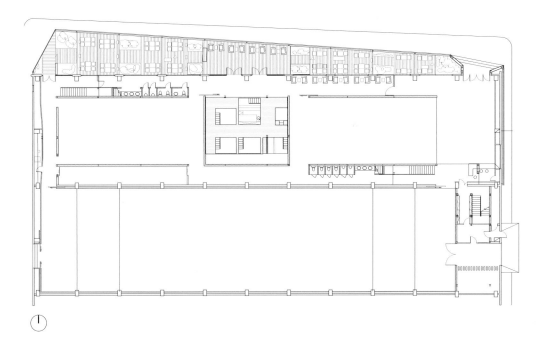

The Baoshan District of Shanghai seems an unlikely site for a new museum. Known mostly for its industry, Baoshan is far from the glossy new developments of other parts of the city. According to the local government, "By 2020, Baoshan will be built into a riverside modern district… compatible with the international metropolis of Shanghai."[41] But a walk through the district today reveals little that could be described as "modern" or "international" among its active and abandoned factories.

The museum's site is the former bottle factory of Shanghai Glass Company. When SGC moved its glassmaking operations to less expensive real estate, its owner decided to transform the site into a more contemporary type of business—the glass-themed G+ Park, with a glass museum as its centerpiece. As a state-owned company, SGC holds unlimited land-use rights to the site, but only if it does not change its industry-related character.

SGC chose logon to develop the museum. The client was looking for a big-statement building to draw a crowd, but logon countered with a different proposal. "The neighborhood at that moment was very messy," says Frank Krueger, creative director of logon. "That led us to the idea of making something quite simple."[42] That simple idea was to convert two of SGC's former factory buildings into exhibition galleries, connect them with a glass-enclosed space, and sandwich them between two new buildings containing an entrance lobby and cafe at the front and glass workshops at the rear. The progression through the museum—new, old, new, old, new—is intentionally evident. The additions are designed as twenty-first-century buildings and the original buildings left almost as found.

The facade of the new entrance is the project's marquee feature. Glass was an obvious choice of material for the designers. After two months of researching glass techniques, logon decided to use U-shaped glass, a standard industry material, in a unique way. Logon coated the inside of each piece of German-made wired security glass (they could not find an equivalent Chinese material) with black enamel, heated the enamel to affix it to the glass, then sandblasted glass-related words in different languages—*slumping, geöffnet, soplado*—to create more than five hundred unique panels. By day the glass bricks form a wordy welcome to the building. When daylight fades, the glass wall is partially backlit, highlighting a scattershot selection of words.

The museum is only part of G+ Park's first phase of development, which also includes a hot-glass show and glass-painting workshop. For its next phase, plans are underway to add a wedding hall and chapel, a high-rise office, commercial facilities, and a glass aquarium, among other things. This smorgasbord of amenities might seem odd to an outsider, but, according to Krueger, providing enough activities to make a visit to Baoshan worthwhile is key to G+'s success. Already SHMOG has become a showpiece for the district. "The Baoshan government is very happy now," says Krueger. "If they have any important visitors coming from Beijing or abroad, they go to the glass museum. This is the future of Baoshan."

Night view
toward entrance

TOP LEFT:
Side view of
entrance lobby

TOP RIGHT:
View of path
between museum
building and
auxiliary building

BOTTOM LEFT:
New glass-
enclosed
exhibition space
between extant
buildings

BOTTOM RIGHT:
Entrance lobby

OPPOSITE

TOP LEFT:
Exhibition gallery

TOP RIGHT:
Main exhibition
hall

BOTTOM LEFT:
First floor plan

BOTTOM RIGHT:
Second floor plan

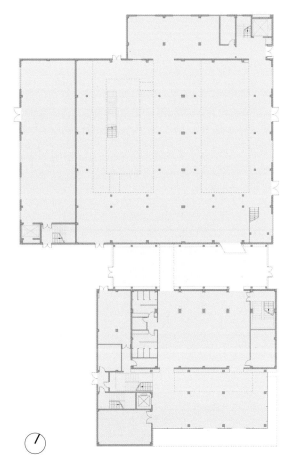
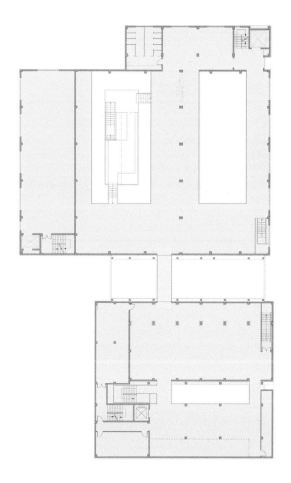

Shanghai Nature Museum evolved out of China's first museum, Siccawei Museum (or Xujiahui Museum or Musée de Zikawei, depending on whom you ask). In 1868 Pierre Heude and his fellow Jesuits created the museum to display Heude's zoological collections.[43] These specimens are now part of the Shanghai Museum of Natural History, housed since 1956 in the 1923 Shanghai Cotton Goods Exchange near Shanghai's Bund.[44] The neoclassical museum retains much of its historic charm. Along with its impressive collection of stuffed mammals and the obligatory dinosaur fossils, its exhibits include a dust-covered diorama of giant jellyfish under miniature junks and a cutaway drawing of a pig indicating which pork parts are used in which Chinese medicines.[45]

Perkins+Will's competition-winning design updates the image of the old museum. The curving, green-roofed, sunken building—renamed the Shanghai Nature Museum—is very twenty-first century. It relocated to a site adjacent to a sculpture garden on prime downtown property, three blocks north of the high-end shopping on West Nanjing Road. "Most of the other competition schemes had a lot more of their area above grade," says Ralph Johnson, design principal of Perkins+Will. "By sinking it below grade, we were able to make it more compatible with the park."[46] Building underground works fine for the exhibits, most of which favor black boxes over natural light. But it gave Perkins+Will problems later in the design process. When a line of Shanghai's ever-expanding subway system was routed under the museum, the project was delayed so the designers could make necessary structural adjustments.

The scheme's form is derived from a nautilus, which Johnson calls "the purest form of nature." The downward-spiraling shape allows the building to "come down to the scale of the park rather than being an object sitting in the park," he says. A courtyard referencing a traditional Chinese mountain water garden fills the spiral's center. Johnson worked with Peter Schaudt of Hoerr Schaudt Landscape Architects to develop its design. The courtyard brings light into the museum's public areas and acts as a visual focus.

In addition to the nautilus, other nature themes include paving meant to suggest tectonic plates and a hydroponic wall on the museum's east facade. The sun-screening wall around the courtyard was influenced by the structure of human cells. It is also meant as an abstraction of Chinese garden screens. "That was the whole idea behind the museum—to bring culture and science and nature together," says Johnson.

Another nature-oriented element is the greening of the building, which includes geothermal heating, evaporative cooling, and rainwater and gray-water collection. The museum is designed to reach China Three-Star green-building designation. It seems no accident that "nature" has replaced "natural history" in the new museum's name. Johnson says his office initiated this greening, but the client was very responsive to the idea. "They see it as part of the exhibits," he says. As of press time, the actual exhibits are yet to be determined. They will certainly include dinosaur fossils from the old Shanghai Museum of Natural History. Hopefully, one or two of Heude's dust-covered mammals will also remain on display.

PERKINS+WILL | SHANGHAI, 2014

SHANGHAI NATURE MUSEUM

TOP:
Rendering of bird's-eye view from south

———

BOTTOM:
Bird's-eye view from south during construction

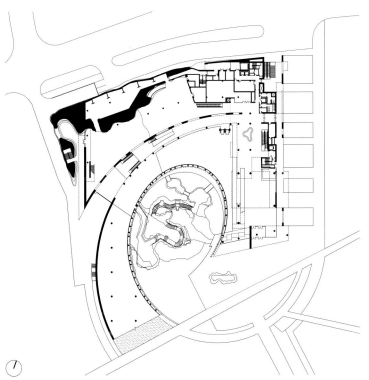

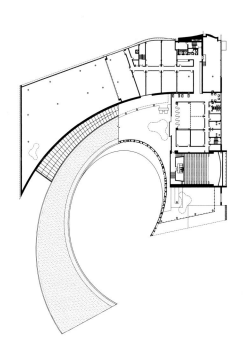

①

Unlike many firms involved in museum design, David Chipperfield Architects is known for subtlety. Its River and Rowing Museum in Henley-on-Thames (1997), Figge Art Museum in Davenport (2005), and The Hepworth Wakefield (2011) use subdued colors and shockingly straight lines in what has been dubbed "neo-minimalist" design.[47] The Liangzhu Museum near Hangzhou exemplifies this approach.

"It's not a complicated building," says Mark Randel, partner of David Chipperfield Architects, Berlin. "It has a simplicity that makes it very authentic."[48] According to Randel, that simplicity came in part from the museum's program, or rather lack of program. When the design was being developed, the museum had no director and a limited agenda. "The program consisted of a total number of square meters and the wish to have three huge, completely dark spaces, because completely dark meant completely flexible," says Randel. "So that was our brief." The lack of a lengthy list of requirements was not a completely bad thing: "It was a nice opportunity to make a sculptural piece of architecture."

That sculpture is a museum laid out as four parallel, rectangular, adjoining bars. The long volumes undulate in plan, as if jockeying for position. Each is fifty-nine feet wide, but each has a different height, giving the sculpture some variation. The bars nestle together on an artificial island on an artificial lake in a park that was once a brownfield site; visitors access the museum via bridges. Randel likens the museum to a rock in the landscape. He says its monolithic design came not only from the bare-bones black-box program "but also the wish to create a very low and very quiet piece of architecture in this park."

This building-cum-sculpture was realized with Iranian travertine facing on a concrete structure. Minimal openings interrupt the long facades, allowing for a scaleless, artistic reading. Inside the museum the light-colored travertine is accented with dark Ipe wood, a hardwood chosen because it, like the stone, ages well. This wood is used for the reception desk and for the thirteen-foot doors that lead from the exhibition rooms to the museum's courtyards.

"I think that the most important aspect [of the museum] is the courtyard," says Randel. Because the project brief called for windowless exhibition rooms, the architects thought visitors might need a bit of light. They cut five courtyards into the plan. These "outside spaces inside" follow "a very Chinese motif," Randel acknowledges. The courtyards bring not only light to the building but also water, plant life, and a museumgoer's best friend—seating.

The courtyards also enhance circulation; visitors can cut through them to deviate from the main museum route. "We wanted people to be able to go from one exhibition room to the next without being exposed to the rain," says Randel. "So we created walkways around each courtyard." Like the building's form, materials, and structure, the design of each courtyard is nothing extraordinary. It is the consistent language and refined execution of all these elements that make the Liangzhu Museum noteworthy. "It's an easy program and a very simple idea that make the building strong," says Randel.

View of
courtyard

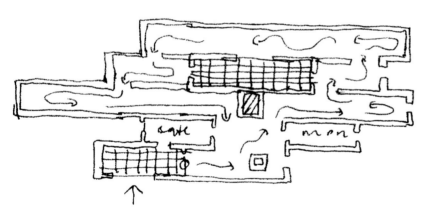

TOP:
View from lake

BOTTOM LEFT:
Sketch of plan

OPPOSITE

BOTTOM RIGHT:
View to courtyard

Details of
travertine facade

TOP:
View to Ipe wood
doors

———

BOTTOM LEFT:
View of sitting
area

———

BOTTOM RIGHT:
View to courtyard

OPPOSITE

TOP:
First floor plan

———

BOTTOM:
Sections

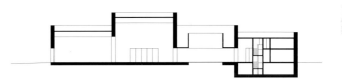

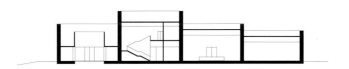

Wang Shu, principal of Amateur Architecture Studio, explains the origin of the old-meets-new Museum of the Imperial Road. "We were commissioned to take charge of the renovation project of [Lirenfang Alley]," he says. "An archaeological excavation had been done there before the construction began, and the ruins of an ancient street were found. I proposed to the mayor that the museum should be the protection of the ruins."[49]

The site of these ruins is on a pedestrian street in Hangzhou, just east of the city's main attraction, West Lake. Wang knows the city well, as it is where he heads China Academy of Art's Architecture Department and where he and his partner and wife, Lu Wenyu, base their Amateur Architecture Studio. "In this historical preservation block, any new building would lead to great controversy," Wang says. "But our idea and way of design, which crosses thousands of years, is apparently beyond controversy." That idea was to borrow a timber construction technique used in ancient local bridges to make two adjoining roofs for the museum. "The street was initiated a thousand years ago," Wang explains. "I chose a wooden bridge structure that originated a thousand years ago." The new roofs—a large one near the street and a smaller one to the rear—form the identity of the museum.

Wang adopted the bridge precedent for both its history and its contemporary effectiveness. "By using small pieces of wood and achieving a big span, the design is very suitable to the archaeological site," says Wang. This does not mean that the roof is a historical re-creation. Its arched structure, made of pine logs with intact bark, is similar to that of the bridges. But its top layer, made of recycled black roof tiles, takes on a contemporary, zigzag profile. "There is natural ventilation between the layers," Wang explains, "a good way of cooling in an area that is extremely hot during the summer."

The museum is difficult to ignore, even when it is closed, as the glass-covered remains of the old road sit in the middle of the current street. Pedestrians can walk around the displays or take a path between the enclosures, which are set at a perfect height for kid-level viewing. A third, modern roof with steel supports juts out over the glass. When the large entry gate is rolled back, visitors can enter the big space: a courtyard under the main roof, with stairs leading down to a closer look at remnants of the old road. An exhibition room on the first floor and a tearoom on the second floor take up the rear. An adjacent concrete tower is used for circulation and contains a private tearoom on the third floor. Both tearooms are currently being used as administrative offices.[50]

A plan to include new works by various artists on Lirenfang Alley has not succeeded as planned. Some projects were constructed but modified by the client; others were canceled outright. But the Museum of the Imperial Road has had an effect, according to Wang. He says, "The long-abandoned street regained its vitality."

TOP:
View toward front facade, with covered remains of ancient street in foreground

BOTTOM:
View from indoor exhibition area toward street

MUSEUM OF THE IMPERIAL ROAD

AMATEUR ARCHITECTURE STUDIO | HANGZHOU, ZHEJIANG, 2009

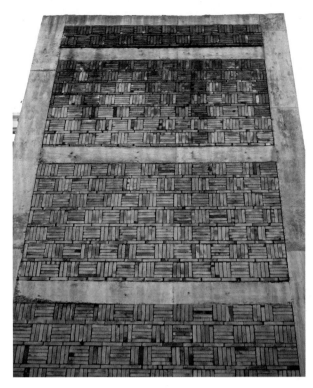

The idea behind MVRDV's design of the China Comic and Animation Museum could not be more direct: speech bubbles. Six connecting bubbles house the project's six programs: entrance, permanent exhibition, theater, library, education center, and an interactive space where visitors can play games with other visitors and with virtual visitors via the Internet. Speech bubbles are familiar to readers of any language. It is an idea, says Shi Wenchian, project manager at MVRDV, that easily won the jury's selection in a 2011 invited competition.[51] Pritzker prize–winning architect and jury member Wang Shu said, "The proposal by MVRDV detours from our previous preconception of architecture. It has a sense of uniqueness and creativeness."[52]

The design may seem ambitious in a country that struggles with construction shortcomings. But it is partly because of the quality of local detailing that MVRDV decided to focus on the big picture. Shi says that after many years of working in China the firm understands what to expect. "We know the reality will be rough," she says. "The shape of the building itself is more important."

This knowledge led MVRDV to reconsider its original proposal for a concrete facade. Local concrete, Shi contends, is both expensive and not of the finest quality. So the designers will use tile to face the bubbles. This is not the ubiquitous white tile of so many preprosperity Chinese buildings, but rather small, locally sourced porcelain tiles set in a system like those used by Antoni Gaudí and Santiago Calatrava on their curved forms.

Materials were not the only consideration in designing the speech bubbles. Siting the rounded forms on stilts in the water of White Horse Lake will be a structural feat. MVRDV is working with engineers from Arup's Shanghai office to figure out the details. Arup came up with a simple solution. While a single speech bubble on one skinny leg would have no stability, together the six bubbles could act like elephants in a circus, leaning on each other for support. The bubbles' steel shells, making up 60 to 70 percent of the total weight, form an exoskeleton. Interior slabs rest on these shells, and the whole sits on concrete legs in the lake. Rounding the forms and elevating the buildings will counteract the force of the wind coming from the direction of the water.

The museum's fire escapes posed a unique challenge. MVRDV sized the routes based on its understanding of local code. The local review board had a different reading and requested more fire escapes, and the building's legs got thicker. The leg for the theater bubble, which required the most fire exits, got especially fat. "We did our best to keep it looking like a speech bubble," says Shi. "As soon as it looked like a muffin, we had to make it smaller."

TOP:
Rendering of view from White Horse Lake

BOTTOM:
Rendering of bird's-eye view

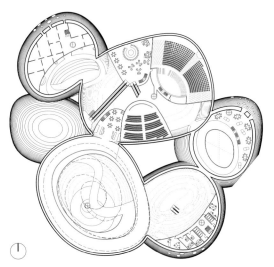

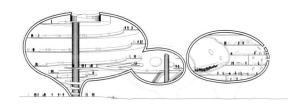

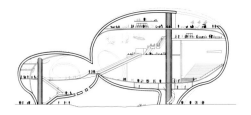

"Boxlike modern buildings are boring," says Wang Shu, principal of Amateur Architecture Studio. "I am more interested in the transformation of the city and in form caused by natural growth."[53] Wang's Ningbo History Museum epitomizes this idea, a big box that has grown up unevenly, its form becoming top-heavy as it expands into the sky. With a footprint of 103,000 square feet and a total footage of 323,000 square feet, the museum is mountainous. Thin cuts into its mass feel like fissures. They create an active roofscape where sloping walls erupt from the visitors' deck. "The roof came from a synthesized feeling," says Wang, "related to the shape of the hills in Chinese traditional water and hill paintings [shan shui] and the spatial form of the destructed traditional villages of this area."

These villages are the source material for the museum's facade. To build its competition-winning design, Amateur Architecture Studio collected bricks and tiles from demolished local buildings and layered them in painterly patterns on the exterior walls. The resulting facade, rooted in both the traditions of Chinese building and contemporary form making, speaks directly to Wang's selection as 2012 Pritzker Architecture Prize Laureate. In announcing the jury's choice, Thomas J. Pritzker stated, "China's unprecedented opportunities for urban planning and design will want to be in harmony with both its long and unique traditions of the past and with its future needs for sustainable development."[54]

Dark bands of collected material highlight the building's summit. "More than forty kinds of bricks, of different eras and sizes, have been used," says Wang. "They vary from dozens of years to hundreds of years old." Reinforced concrete forms the museum's structure and sometimes pops out as the facade surface. This material has a less lofty origin than the historic masonry. Concrete was used, says Wang, "because it is the lowest-cost way of building structure in China." It also ensures that the museum is waterproof.

Amateur Architecture Studio used this same masonry technique in other projects, including its Ningbo Tengtou Pavilion for Expo 2010 Shanghai. The Shanghai pavilion included installations specific to the five senses. These make explicit what the Ningbo History Museum only suggests—that architecture can be a sensual experience. When asked about this sensuality, Wang says, "It's very difficult to express with words. One needs to experience it on-site."

The logic of the museum is truly experiential. It has a different sense than a building calculated according to some proportional system or for strict functionality. Wang describes the fenestration: "I set the windows based on a Chinese traditional pattern, mainly to keep the abstract feeling of the elevation." The manner in which thin horizontal and vertical slits break up the heavy wall seems more like a rhythm than a pattern.

The museum's interior similarly follows an irregular logic (and confirms Wang's dislike of box-like modern buildings). Walls and a grand stairway to the roof deck cut at diagonals into the rectangular perimeter wall. These unexpected angles reinforce Wang's preference for "form caused by natural growth." Asked about the influence of nature on the design, Wang says, "It mainly comes from my travel experience in the natural mountains and waters." Wang's office is based in Hangzhou, a city known throughout China for West Lake and its scenic beauty.

The Ningbo History Museum has become the image of Amateur Architecture Studio, the most recognizable work of the practice. When asked why the building connects with so many people, Wang replies, "Because it's a place that keeps people's memory." This may be a material memory, a connection to the sensuality of old brick that is absent from many new Chinese constructions. It may be the memory of Chinese mountains and water, visited in trips to the countryside or viewed in shan shui. Or it might be a more primordial memory, something intangible that nonetheless feels right. "It not only keeps people's memory," says Wang, "but also gives people hope."

View of roof terrace

TOP:
View from
northwest

CENTER:
View from
southwest

BOTTOM:
Detail of facade
showing windows
"based on a
Chinese traditional
pattern"

OPPOSITE

Interior stairs

OPPOSITE

TOP:
Second floor plan

CENTER:
East elevation

Views of roof   BOTTOM:
terrace   Sections

EAST 142

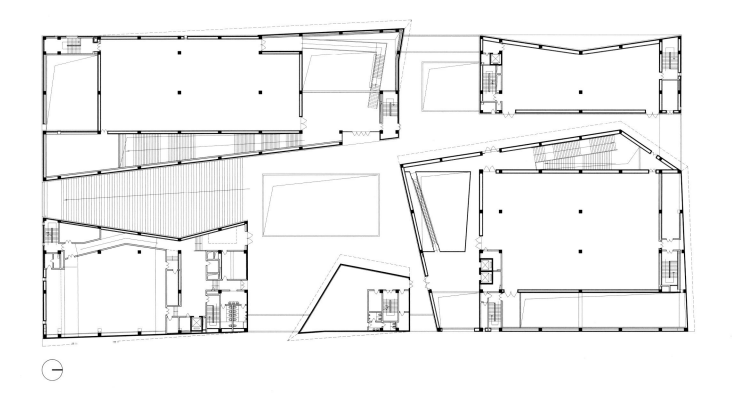

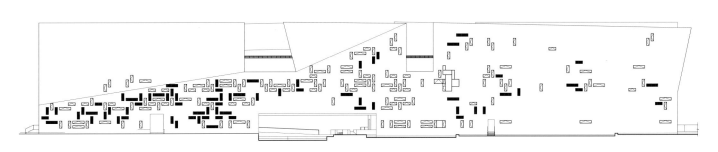

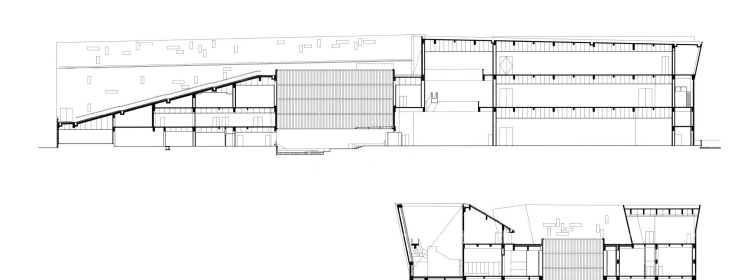

"Normally, when you walk into a building, you feel its scale," says Pei Zhu, principal of his eponymous studio. "You know the ceiling, you know the wall, you know the floor—you know everything. And then you basically have no [room for] imagination. But here you have to think."[1]

It may be surprising that Zhu is describing his OCT Design Museum, a building that could be read as the epitome of building as object, rather than as a scaleless environment. Its stainless-steel shell forms a picturesque body, a curvy contrast to the urban grid of Shenzhen. Studio Pei-Zhu's website states: "The building form resembles the smooth stone that's been cast from the shore and displaced in this saturated urban setting."[2] But for Zhu, "If we see it more like a pebble or like a UFO, it doesn't matter."

What matters, says Zhu, is the museum's boundless interior. "Why do people need to realize the real scale? Consider people walking on the street compared to swimming in the water. When you are swimming, you feel totally free. You feel sort of surreal, and you also feel the beautiful moment. It feels like flight. This is the kind of experience I want to catch. I want to turn people's perceptions upside down."

Zhu finds precedent for this idea. "The Chinese always talk about this: something must have a limit, but actually sometimes things are unlimited," he says. "We can see this as an object building. But once you get inside, you're going to feel infinity. That limit and limitlessness follows Chinese philosophy."

To achieve this limitlessness, the OCT Design Museum presents an egglike interior, vast swaths of white drywall spotted with triangular pinhole windows. A circulation core disconnected from the perimeter walls links the first-floor lobby and cafe to the second- and third-floor exhibition spaces. "A lot of the floor area is not attached to the shell in order to make this space flow better," says Zhu. In this scaleless center, he seems to have been given free reign for his spatial exploration.

Still, that big, silver bubble of the facade demands attention. Beyond the interior space and its white lining are layers of steel structure, insulation, and stainless-steel panels. "You can see the structure is so light," says Zhu. "This shell is very thin." Lightness is important to Zhu. Speaking about his Yi Garden installation at the 2010 Venice Biennale, Zhu said, "If we use minimal building materials, our architecture will take on notions that can achieve an artistic value."[3]

Zhu designed the pebble-like (or UFO-like) shape of the OCT Design Museum, and his staff standardized the exterior metal panels on a computer in order to make it affordable. The museum uses eleven sizes of panels for the steel cladding, but around 85 percent of them are the same size.

Joining these panels to create a seamless surface was a difficult but crucial job, according to Zhu. "This building has a very clear shape, but once you use a softer, reflecting material, then the profile starts to blend, to melt with the sky and with the landscape," he says. "Then clear things start to become unclear. Sometimes you feel the building is here, sometimes you feel its really soft dialogue with its surroundings. I think this makes this building seem less permanent."

Zhu would like the museum to be read as a temporary construction. "I feel this is a real challenge right now. Architecture is always permanent, is always driven by functionality," he says. "Once the building can be mobile, once it can be invisible, then people will not feel the building is so solid, occupying too much space." He sees temporality as a strategy for a new, sustainable direction for architecture. "If I can recycle everything, maybe this museum today is here, maybe tomorrow in Tiananmen Square or in Paris—wherever." For now, Zhu's steel stone sits squarely—or, rather, roundly—in Shenzhen.

View of "limitless" interior

OPPOSITE

Views from plaza   Views of interior

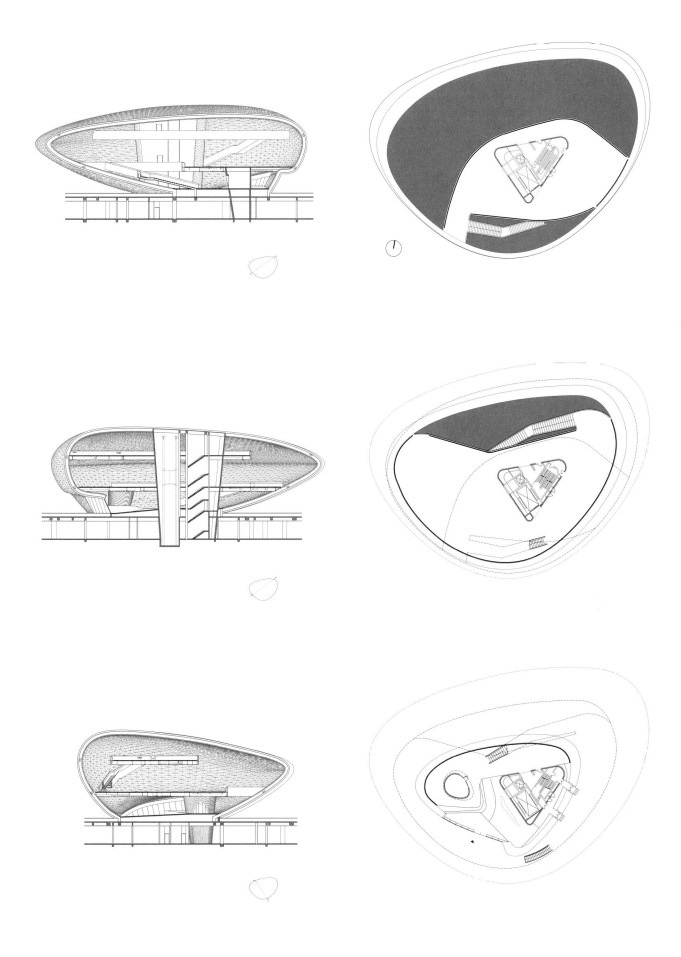

The huge success story of Dafen Art Village—what has been called "one of the most uniquely surreal, creative, and economically sustainable" phenomena in Shenzhen—began small.[4] In 1989 the Hong Kong businessman Huang Jiang set up a studio in Buji, an industrial district on the outskirts of Shenzhen, to teach local artists how to reproduce famous oil paintings to sell in China and abroad. Soon enough, migrant workers came to the village to paint rather than going to factories to assemble. They took up brushes and re-created *The Last Supper*s and *The Starry Night*s by the thousands. By 2008 Dafen supported fifteen thousand artists and eight hundred art-related businesses.[5] In 2010 sales of Dafen art reached RMB 500 million (USD 7.5 million).[6]

Dafen's growth was a bottom-up affair, unlike the government-sponsored development that marks most of Shenzhen's success.[7] Yet in 2005 the local government stepped in and held a competition for a museum to celebrate the village's cultural success. "The reason for the government to sponsor the project is because Dafen Art Village turned out to be a creative business," says Wang Hui, principal of Urbanus Architecture & Design. "The government had a good intent to elevate this business into something higher. But this kind of change would totally ruin the business."[8] Dafen's success depended on cheap rent, cheap labor, and cheap selling prices. Wang recounts buying a painting in Dafen and bringing it home, where he found that "framing in Beijing was much more expensive than the painting." If the art village's working model changed, so too might its success.

Urbanus's Dafen Art Museum attempts to maintain the village's character, "to preserve this kind of automatic business and automatic urban setting, which is totally opposite to today's high-rises and well-planned development," says Wang. "This is spontaneous and provisional planning." Urbanus saw the museum as a center of activity rather than a staid institution. The ground floor would allow for a covered market for local vendors; the top floor would provide spaces for workshops and artists' studios. The middle of the building would contain exhibition spaces for local work.

The museum's design addresses the specific urban quality of Dafen. Its given site was one-tenth of the village's area. "If we had built something really big, it would totally have ruined the existing fabric," says Wang. Instead, Urbanus kept the building to 183,000 square feet and left a large open plaza around it. It ran pathways through the structure to connect corners of the site and manage bi-level terrain. Urbanus used the urban grid as an aesthetic device. It abstracted the rooftop plan of local buildings and placed a similar pattern of squares on the museum's roof, where they are incised into the surface or pop up as light wells. A map of the village, titled on an angle, appears on the facade. Some blocks are rendered as windows, others as light-colored indentations into the dark outer concrete surface. Urbanus planned that the panels would eventually contain art. Wang says this facade is "like a canvas to be filled later on, so this building can grow with the village."

Urbanus has had mixed success in transforming their intentions into built realities. The museum has become an occasional site for local artists. Its plaza was used to gather 507 painters to produce a giant version of the *Mona Lisa* for the World Expo 2010 Shanghai, while its exhibition galleries showcased local artists and their original, nonreproduction works in the 2011 Dafen Oil Painting Fair.[9] The blank canvas of the facade has received some art, thanks in part to an international mural exhibition in 2010.

The planned on-site shops, on the other hand, did not materialize. "Actually the whole village is a big shopping mall," says Wang, "so it's not necessary for the museum to have specific shops." In addition, the museum's management has hindered Urbanus's plan to open pathways through the building. "Even though the museum may not completely realize what we planned," says Wang, "still it's a very good example of showing how a museum can be part of a community and how it can relate to more people, not just well-educated people. In this sense it's unique."

Roof plaza

TOP:
Bird's-eye view

BOTTOM LEFT:
View from south
with bridge to roof
plaza

BOTTOM RIGHT:
Skylit gallery

OPPOSITE

TOP:
Site plan

BOTTOM:
Section

SOUTH CENTRAL 152

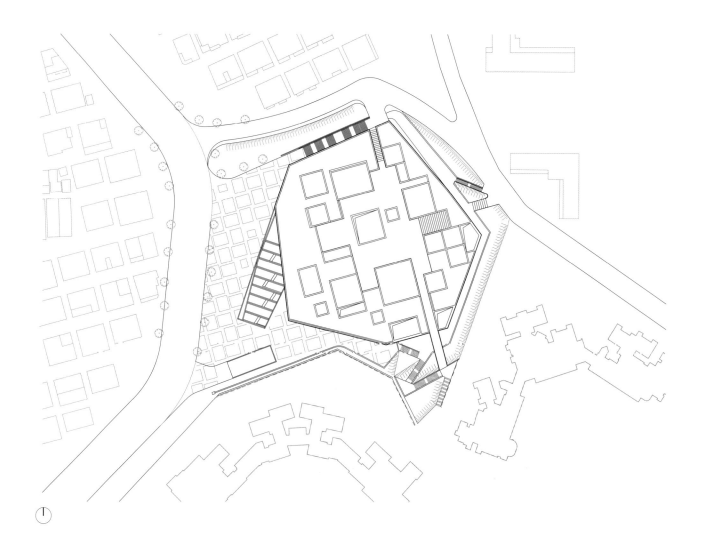

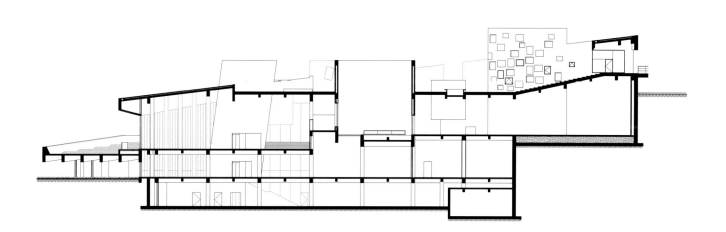

"We never do one-liner architecture," says Wolf D. Prix, design principal and CEO of Coop Himmelb(l)au. "There are always a lot of stories behind it that make it so intense."[10] This might explain the complex forms Prix and his colleagues have been designing since 1968. He mentions the plethora of considerations that influenced his Museum of Contemporary Art and Planning Exhibition (MOCAPE), including code-driven setbacks, visitor movement, ecological construction, and Mars's inner moon, Phobos. The resulting building—a 1.2-million-square-foot sculpture—encapsulates an artist's view of making architecture.

Prix brings this complex building to a complex place—Shenzhen. As China's first Special Economic Zone, the city is a hugely successful experiment in China's *gaige kaifang* (reform and opening). Its financial centers and industrial parks seem ever-present in the news, and the new cultural center in its Futian District embodies hopes for another kind of notoriety. This site, anchored by a behemoth civic center, includes MOCAPE and four accordant buildings: a cultural center by Arata Isozaki, a bookstore by Kisho Kurakawa, and an as-yet-to-be-built opera house and youth activity hall.[11]

Rather than turn its back on this mélange, MOCAPE will connect to its neighboring structures and even offers a platform for viewing them. "The concept of our architecture is to create synergy between private and public space," says Prix. The building rotates toward the cultural center, turning its head to acknowledge its community.

The museum's dual programs affect its composite form. "It's a space for information," says Prix. "On the one side you have information about the city, on the other the newest movement of Chinese art." Coop Himmelb(l)au rendered the former (PE) as an open, rotating stack of platforms and the latter (MOCA) as a closed, rectilinear box. These two sit across an open platform atop a thirty-three-foot-high plinth. "There is a pathway going through both museums," says Prix. "You can walk around without going directly to the exhibition. It's kind of a three-dimensional Chinese garden where you can see a lot of attractions."

The whole is encased in insulated glass and then a layer of perforated stainless steel. "What we are going for is a glass box protected by different shapes of blinds in order to keep the sun out or to bring light in," says Prix. He adds, "The metal gives the whole building the monolithic character that I really wanted." In fact, Coop Himmelb(l)au refers to the project as an "Urban Monolith."[12]

Between the two museums is the "cloud," whose amorphous form Prix attributes to experimentation with the shape of Phobos. The cloud began, as Coop Himmelb(l)au designs historically have begun, with handmade models. Then parametric software took over. The space is still in development and may be used as a teahouse, an auditorium, a restaurant, an information center, or some combination of the above. Whatever unfolds, Prix insists that the cloud will "build up a synergy between the two museums." Conceptually, this cloud is not so different from Coop Himmelb(l)au's germinative 1968 Cloud project for Vienna, "living forms for the future."[13] Prix's early artistic vision for Austria may have been unbuildable, but that for China is being built.

Rendering of
bird's-eye view

MUSEUM OF CONTEMPORARY ART AND PLANNING EXHIBITION

COOP HIMMELB(L)AU | SHENZHEN, GUANGDONG, 2015

OPPOSITE

TOP:
Rendering of view
from plaza

CENTER AND
BOTTOM:
Renderings of
interior view
toward the cloud

TOP LEFT:
Model showing
layers of the
program

TOP RIGHT:
Concept model

BOTTOM:
Section

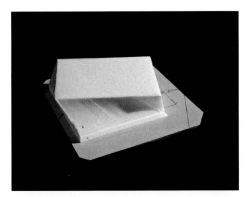

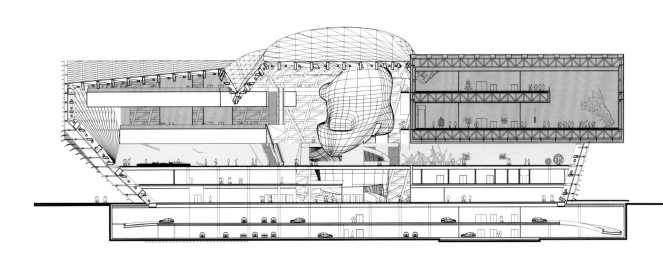

"Although it's a museum in China, it's not really a museum in China," says Billie Tsien, principal of Tod Williams Billie Tsien Architects (TWBTA). "It's an anomaly."[14] She is talking about the Asia Society Hong Kong (ASHK), a new museum on a 3.2-acre site in Admiralty. "This building was generated from America, in a certain way." Not only ASHK's architects but also its founding organization hail from New York. As the first branch of a US museum to be built in China, ASHK cannot help but be an outsider.[15]

But the museum is anomalous in a more significant way. "Hong Kong is just festooned with towers," says Tod Williams, principal of TWBTA.[16] Land is money here, and so developers build skyscrapers. In the middle of this, ASHK built a groundscraper. "The topography of the museum site is as vertical as the palm of my hand," says Williams. His palm is not unusually bumpy, but its hills and valleys make his point. "So the museum is not really scraping the ground, because the ground is undulating. But it's a horizontal building in a vertical landscape."

Williams offers a conceptual rationale for the project's horizontality. "In the 1800s, the British took this hillside and carved a flat table out of it," he says. "The flat table became our concept. That's the horizontality we're talking about." There is another, more practical reason behind TWBTA's low-lying design: its site condition. ASHK is built from the remains of the Explosives Magazine Compound, a gunpowder-processing and storage center used by the British from the mid-nineteenth century until the 1980s.[17] The new museum reuses four low extant buildings. Magazine A, built between 1863 and 1868, has been converted into a gallery. Magazine B, added between 1905 and 1907, is now a theater. A laboratory (contemporary with Magazine A) and the GG Block (from the late 1940s) currently serve as offices.[18] "The buildings themselves are museological artifacts," says Williams.

TWBTA's insertions are minimally invasive. Tsien talks about reusing Magazine A. "The gallery space in a certain way was pre-determined because it made use of a building that had eight-foot-thick granite walls and a vaulted series of rooms," she says. "Because it's a heritage building, we essentially kept these chambers. So it was really about trying to clean things up and make them well lit." What the architects did add can be removed easily to return the building to its original state.

"The huge thing is the invisible thing: all the mechanical systems have been put into a gigantic vault, which is below grade," Tsien says. She mentions that other heritage buildings in Hong Kong have large mechanical blocks on or next to them and exposed electrical work. "Here we tried to keep the power of the buildings and hide all the things that are needed to make the buildings work."

In addition to its renovation work for ASHK, TWBTA designed a new multipurpose pavilion. This rectangular building with a landscaped roof deck can be used for exhibitions, performances, and business meetings. It includes the AMMO Café, which, according to its interior designers, was inspired by the history of the explosives compound and the Jean-Luc Godard film *Alphaville*.[19] For the new pavilion, "We were very interested in using materials from China," says Tsien. Black granite and gray stonecutters granite from Hong Kong's Stonecutters Island are used as background stones. In the foreground is Mist Green marble from Shanxi. "The one we chose felt like a jungle," says Williams. As the museum site already had four buildings with four distinct architectural languages, TWBTA wanted their new building to be "not so strange." Choosing a stone that fit in with the museum's lush subtropical surroundings kept it simple.

A covered pathway connects the pavilion to its historic neighbors. It zigzags through the site, around existing trees and a population of bats. The long, elevated, sloping form dominates the landscape. So, too, do two large berms built between 1853 and 1910 by the British to help prevent landslides caused by gunpowder mishaps.[20] "The berms are very powerful," says Tsien. "They're massive buildings unto themselves." Though the ASHK program did not insist that these structures be kept, TWBTA found value in them. "We used the platform [set by the berms] to establish the rooftop of the pavilion."

The subdued design of Asia Society Hong Kong—reusing historical buildings with minimal changes, choosing materials that disappear into the landscape, and tiptoeing around trees and bats—may seem an anomaly in the rush of extravagant museums in China. Then again, Hong Kong is an anomaly. "Hong Kong is a world unto itself," says Tsien. "China is interested in nation building, and part of that idea is establishing cultural institutions. People in Hong Kong don't really consider themselves part of *China* China. They're their own thing."

Aerial view with heritage buildings at top, zigzagging covered pathway at center, and new pavilion at bottom

TOP:
View of roof
terrace against the
Hong Kong skyline

OPPOSITE

BOTTOM LEFT:
View of exterior
stair to roof terrace
and water feature

TOP:
View of pathway
from roof terrace

BOTTOM RIGHT:
View of lower
level of pathway

BOTTOM:
View of pavilion
from covered
pathway

TOP:
Walkway through
a berm at the
heritage site

BOTTOM LEFT:
Arrival at former
laboratory now
used as offices

BOTTOM RIGHT:
Gallery interior

OPPOSITE

TOP LEFT:
Plan of ground
level of lower site

TOP RIGHT:
Plan of ground
level of upper site

BOTTOM:
Section through
covered pathway

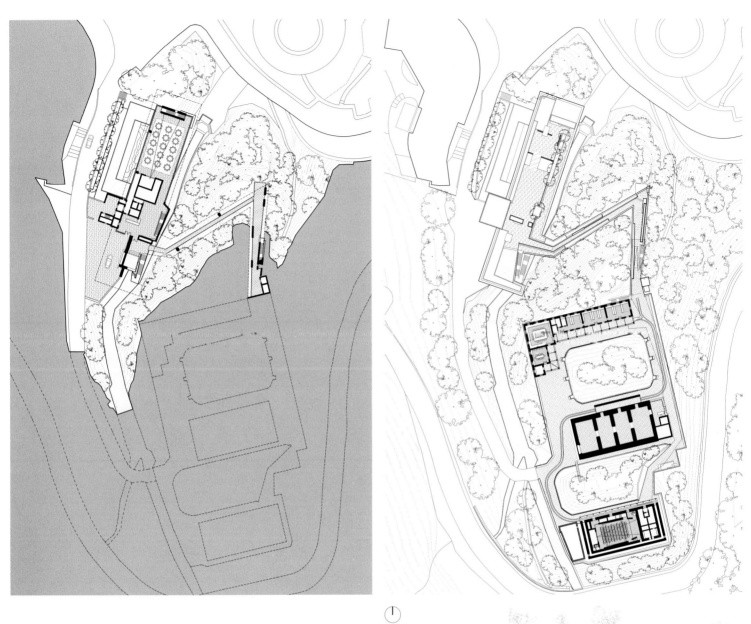

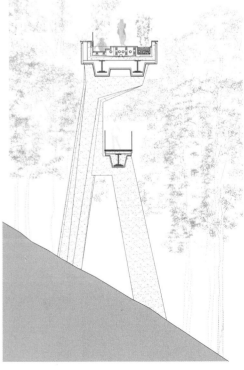

On a site-seeking trip for the Macao Science Center (MSC), Li Chung Pei, principal of Pei Partnership Architects, and I. M. Pei, his father, were given the choice of a few possible locations. According to the younger Pei, one stood out—a site at the southeast edge of the Peninsula of Macao (or Macau), across the Pearl River Estuary from Taipa and Coloane, with a view to Macau Tower.[21] In fact, it was not yet a site, but a location that could be extended into the water through land reclamation. As a prominent entry point to Macao's Outer Harbour, it was a look-at-me site en route to Macao's more looked-at sites, such as Sands's $2.4 billion Venetian resort and casino.[22] And it called for an exceptional museum.

The resulting MSC is a trio of aluminum-clad, geometrically strong buildings. It is not clear whether the dome-shaped planetarium, fanlike convention center, and conical exhibition center simply continue the high-modernist geometries of so many of I. M. Pei's museums or rather are meant to appeal to children, MSC's main clientele. According to Li Chung Pei, the forms' purpose was threefold: to create a landmark on the prominent site, to express the center's functional programs, and to provide an interesting interior experience for visitors.

A dome for a planetarium and a fan for an auditorium might be expected. But a cone for an exhibition space? "The tilted cone came from the idea of how visitors would move through the exhibition spaces," says Pei. He thought a ramp would provide the "most exciting" experience. The asymmetrical cone formed by this ramp resembles an upside-down Solomon R. Guggenheim Museum. Its central atrium under an angled oculus allows visitors a light-filled release from MSC's fourteen exhibition rooms. Visitors can ascend the ramp or ride an interior elevator to an observation deck. Or they can head directly to the view via an exterior escalator and bridge. The observation deck is no Macau Tower (no bungee jumping here), but it does offer a 360-degree view without the $15 price tag.[23]

The cone is a simple concrete structure. Its interior is covered mostly in drywall to permit easy renovation for MSC's changing exhibitions. Except for the ramp, there are no bells and whistles inside; grand gestures were reserved for the exterior, where they have the most impact. Dramatic forms, oversized circulation, and shiny aluminum cladding vie for attention on the skyline. In MSC's bid to compete with Macao's more popular tourist attractions, this emphasis is understandable.

View of escalator and bridge to exhibition hall

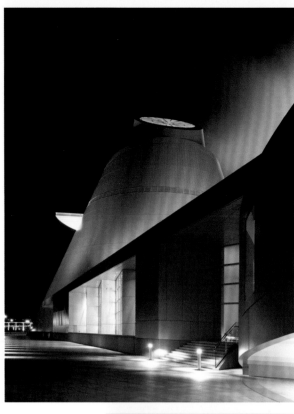

TOP LEFT:
Night view toward
exhibition hall

OPPOSITE

TOP RIGHT:
Interior ramp
and elevator of
exhibition hall

TOP:
Rendering of view
west from Macao
Science Center
toward Macau
Tower

BOTTOM LEFT:
Detail of bridge
to exhibition hall

CENTER:
West–east section

BOTTOM RIGHT:
View from ramp of
exhibition hall

BOTTOM:
Site plan

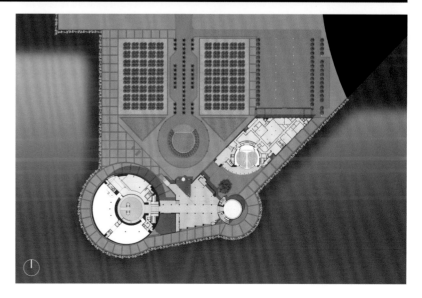

Guangdong Museum by Rocco Design Architects joins a library by Nikken Sekkei, a children's activity center by Steffian Bradley Architects, and a much-discussed opera house by Zaha Hadid Architects to form a new cultural center in Guangdong's Zhujiang New Town. Rocco Design won an invited competition—which included powerhouses like Peter Eisenman, Coop Himmelb(l)au, UNStudio, Hans Hollein, and Eric Owen Moss—to garner the commission. When the Hong Kong–based firm entered the 2003 competition, Zhujiang New Town was a clean slate, a barren, flat riverside parcel. The architects did have an inkling of Hadid's design for the project just west of theirs—enough to know that her opera hall would have an organic shape. "Rocco purposefully did the opposite," says Derrick Tsang, director of Rocco Design Architects. "We wanted to have a dialogue with the opera house—not a contrasting but a balancing dialogue."[24]

The architects' response to Hadid's "two pebbles" opera house is square in plan and rectangular in elevation. "Rocco thought that the Guangdong Museum, being a building that would house a lot of local crafts and treasures, should itself be seen as a treasure box," explains Tsang. The museum's four main exhibition halls show Lingnan (southern Chinese) history, natural history, art, and temporary exhibitions. Its five stories and approximately 721,000 square feet make it a very big box.

"Some of the references we used are the lacquer box and ivory balls," says Tsang, referring to the intricately layered and sculpted Chinese artifacts. "What we like about these is that they have a similar concept to the museum. We think the museum should have different layers housing different things." From outside in, these layers include the facade, exhibition spaces, circulation, and a central atrium. Visitors pop up into the center of the box after walking under its bulk. The museum is suspended from a large space frame with seventy-two-foot cantilevers. "By elevating the museum and making the entrance below the soffit, hopefully there is a monumental experience for visitors walking from the edge of the landscape," Tsang says. Rocco Design conceived the rolling landscape as a silk cloth unfolding to expose the treasure box.

The lacquer box and ivory balls have not only spatial but also formal design implications. The rectangular facade's defining features are the incisions into its aluminum panels, which could be read as ancient carvings.[25] These cuts are sometimes glazed and sometimes filled in, depending on the contents of the exhibition space behind them. Some have louvers; some admit mechanical and engineering systems. Each cut is unique. In addition, there are three facade projections that highlight specific areas, such as the VIP reception room. At night the depressions and protrusions are lit from within, accentuating the depth of the outside layer.

Rocco Design used simple means to achieve the facade's effect. "There's nothing unusual about the material for the museum," Tsang says. "We simply maximized the potential of the material, using very simple technology. Building the project in China, we knew the workmanship would be a tricky thing to control." (Hadid's neighboring opera house, while lauded for its design, has been criticized for the "abysmal" quality of some of its construction.)[26] Tsang and his team understood that architects in mainland China typically only act as consultants during a project's construction, which is managed instead by a local design institute. They chose aluminum, GRC panels, and energy-efficient glass for the facade because those materials are common to Chinese construction and easily obtainable from local manufacturers. Tsang does not seem to regret the missed opportunity to try something more radical. "I think what is strong about the museum is the actual concept," he says. "For a museum, spatial experience is more important than fancy materials or technology."

View from facade toward Canton Tower

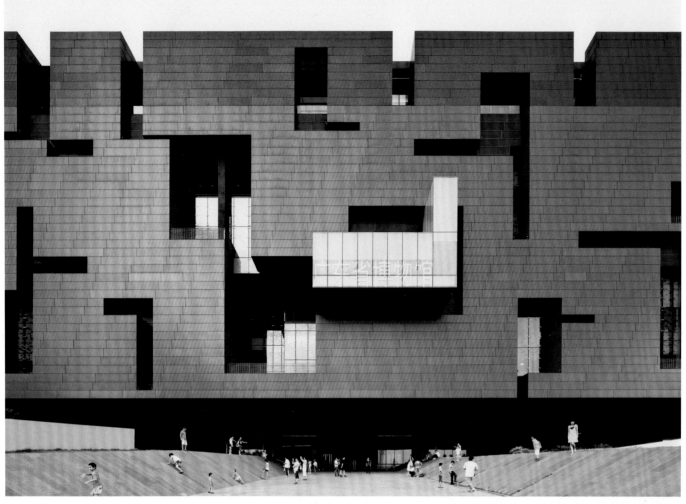

TOP:
View of west
entrance

———

BOTTOM:
Rendering of
bird's-eye view
from southwest
corner

OPPOSITE

Detail of bridge